TRISTAN & ISOLDE

THE WARRIOR AND THE PRINCESS

A BRITISH LEGEND

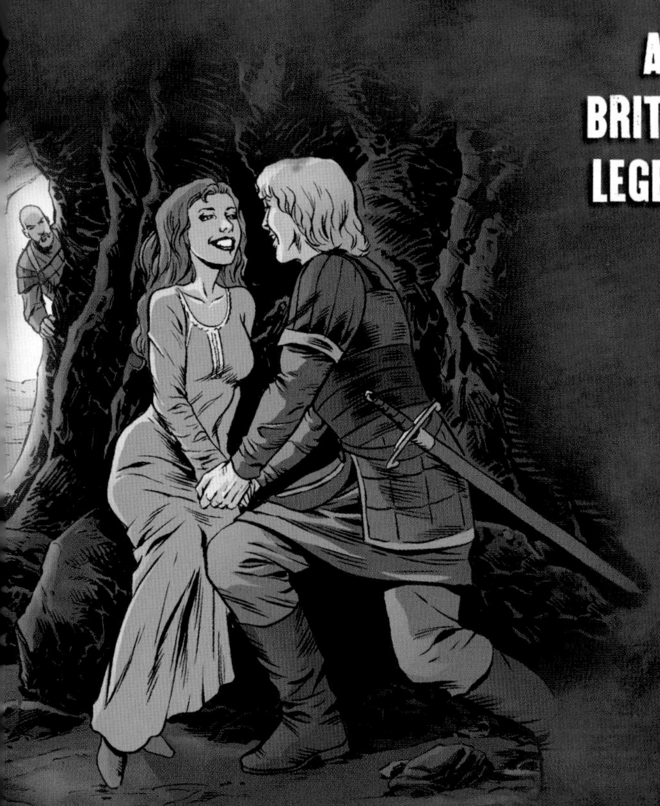

JEFF LIMKE

PENCILS AND INKS BY
RON RANDALL

ADAPTED FROM
CELTIC MYTHOLOGY
AND FROM
SIR THOMAS MALORY'S
LE MORTE D'ARTHUR

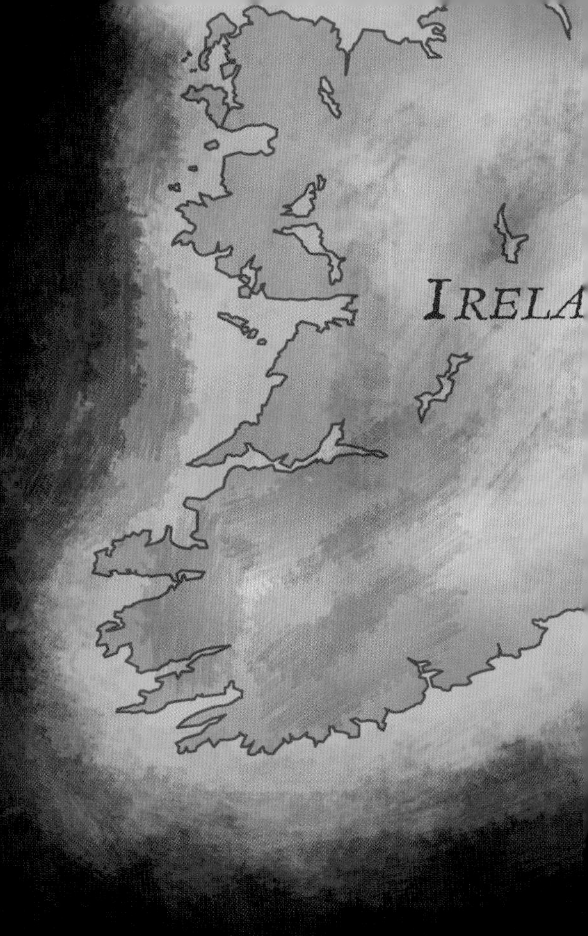
IRELA

TRISTAN & ISOLDE

THE WARRIOR AND THE PRINCESS

A BRITISH LEGEND

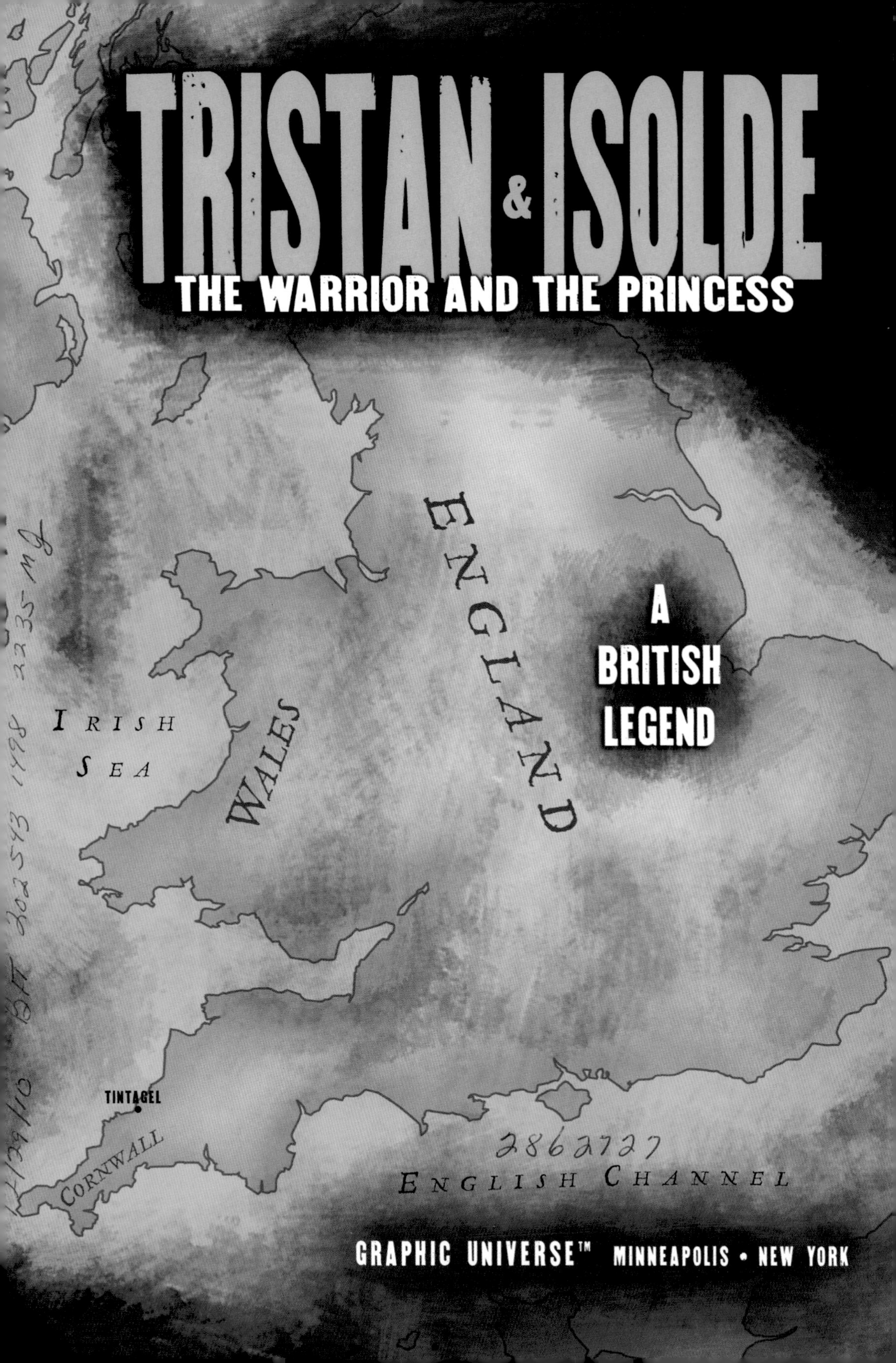
ENGLAND
IRISH SEA
WALES
TINTAGEL
CORNWALL
ENGLISH CHANNEL

GRAPHIC UNIVERSE™ MINNEAPOLIS • NEW YORK

THE STORY OF TRISTAN AND ISOLDE DRAWS ON MANY INFLUENCES FROM THE ANCIENT CELTIC FOLKLORE AND MYTHOLOGY OF WALES, CORNWALL, AND BRITTANY. IN THE HIGH MIDDLE AGES (ABOUT A.D. 1100 TO 1300), THE LEGEND OF THEIR ROMANCE JOINED THE LARGE COLLECTION OF TALES ABOUT KING ARTHUR AND HIS KNIGHTS OF THE ROUND TABLE.

TRISTAN & ISOLDE'S THEME OF TWO YOUNG PEOPLE CAUGHT BETWEEN LOVE AND DUTY WAS COMMON IN MEDIEVAL ROMANCES. FEW PEOPLE IN THAT ERA MARRIED FOR LOVE. MOST MARRIAGES WERE ARRANGED BY PARENTS TO INCREASE A FAMILY'S WEALTH, STATUS, OR SECURITY. YOUNG PEOPLE UNDERSTOOD THEIR DUTY TO THEIR FAMILIES, AND MOST NEVER EXPECTED TO BE ABLE TO CHOOSE THEIR OWN SPOUSES. YET THE THEME OF LOSING A TRUE LOVE AND BEING FORCED TO MARRY SOMEONE ELSE WAS POPULAR. IT REMAINED SO FOR CENTURIES, FEATURED IN WORKS RANGING FROM WILLIAM SHAKESPEARE'S SIXTEENTH-CENTURY PLAY ROMEO AND JULIET TO F. SCOTT FITZGERALD'S MODERN AMERICAN NOVEL THE GREAT GATSBY.

STORY BY JEFF LIMKE

PENCILS AND INKS BY RON RANDALL

COLORING BY HI-FI DESIGN

LETTERING BY MARSHALL DILLON
AND TERRI DELGADO

CONSULTANT: THERESA KRIER, PH.D.,
MACALESTER COLLEGE

Graphic Universe™
A division of Lerner Publishing Group, Inc.
241 First Avenue North
Minneapolis, MN 55401 U.S.A.

Website address: www.lernerbooks.com

Library of Congress Cataloging-in-Publication Data

Limke, Jeff.
    Tristan & Isolde : the warrior and the princess : a British legend ; adapted by Jeff Limke from Celtic mythology and from Sir Thomas Malory's Le morte d'Arthur ; illustrations by Ron Randall.
       p.   cm.
    Includes index.
    ISBN-13: 978-0-8225-7526-9 (lib. bdg. : alk. paper)
    1. Graphic novels. I. Randall, Ron. II. Title: Tristan and Isolde.
PN6727.L53T75 2008
741.5'973—dc22   2007018582

Manufactured in the United States of America
1 2 3 4 5 6 - DP - 13 12 11 10 09 08

TABLE OF CONTENTS

A TREACHEROUS QUEST . . . 6

HEALING A HERO . . . 10

A WEDDING IN CORNWALL . . . 15

FORBIDDEN LOVE . . . 19

TRISTAN RETURNS . . . 27

KNIGHT-ERRANT . . . 31

LOVERS REUNITED . . . 37

GLOSSARY AND PRONUNCIATION GUIDE . . . 46

FURTHER READING AND WEBSITES . . . 47

CREATING *TRISTAN & ISOLDE* . . . 47

INDEX . . . 48

ABOUT THE AUTHOR AND THE ARTIST . . . 48

A TREACHEROUS QUEST

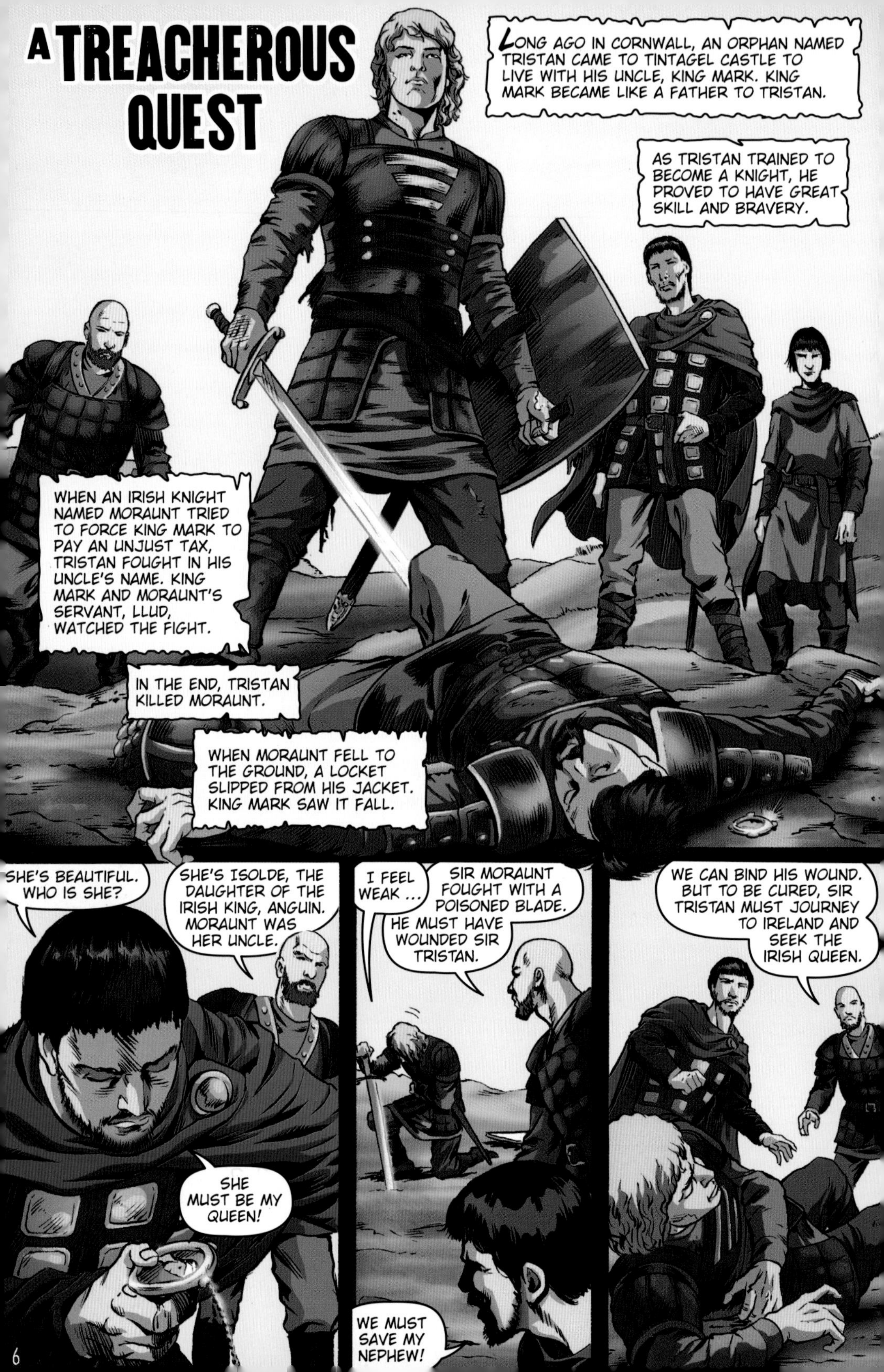
LONG AGO IN CORNWALL, AN ORPHAN NAMED TRISTAN CAME TO TINTAGEL CASTLE TO LIVE WITH HIS UNCLE, KING MARK. KING MARK BECAME LIKE A FATHER TO TRISTAN.
AS TRISTAN TRAINED TO BECOME A KNIGHT, HE PROVED TO HAVE GREAT SKILL AND BRAVERY.
WHEN AN IRISH KNIGHT NAMED MORAUNT TRIED TO FORCE KING MARK TO PAY AN UNJUST TAX, TRISTAN FOUGHT IN HIS UNCLE'S NAME. KING MARK AND MORAUNT'S SERVANT, LLUD, WATCHED THE FIGHT.
IN THE END, TRISTAN KILLED MORAUNT.
WHEN MORAUNT FELL TO THE GROUND, A LOCKET SLIPPED FROM HIS JACKET. KING MARK SAW IT FALL.
SHE'S BEAUTIFUL. WHO IS SHE?
SHE'S ISOLDE, THE DAUGHTER OF THE IRISH KING, ANGUIN. MORAUNT WAS HER UNCLE.
SHE MUST BE MY QUEEN!
I FEEL WEAK ...
SIR MORAUNT FOUGHT WITH A POISONED BLADE.
HE MUST HAVE WOUNDED SIR TRISTAN.
WE MUST SAVE MY NEPHEW!
WE CAN BIND HIS WOUND. BUT TO BE CURED, SIR TRISTAN MUST JOURNEY TO IRELAND AND SEEK THE IRISH QUEEN.

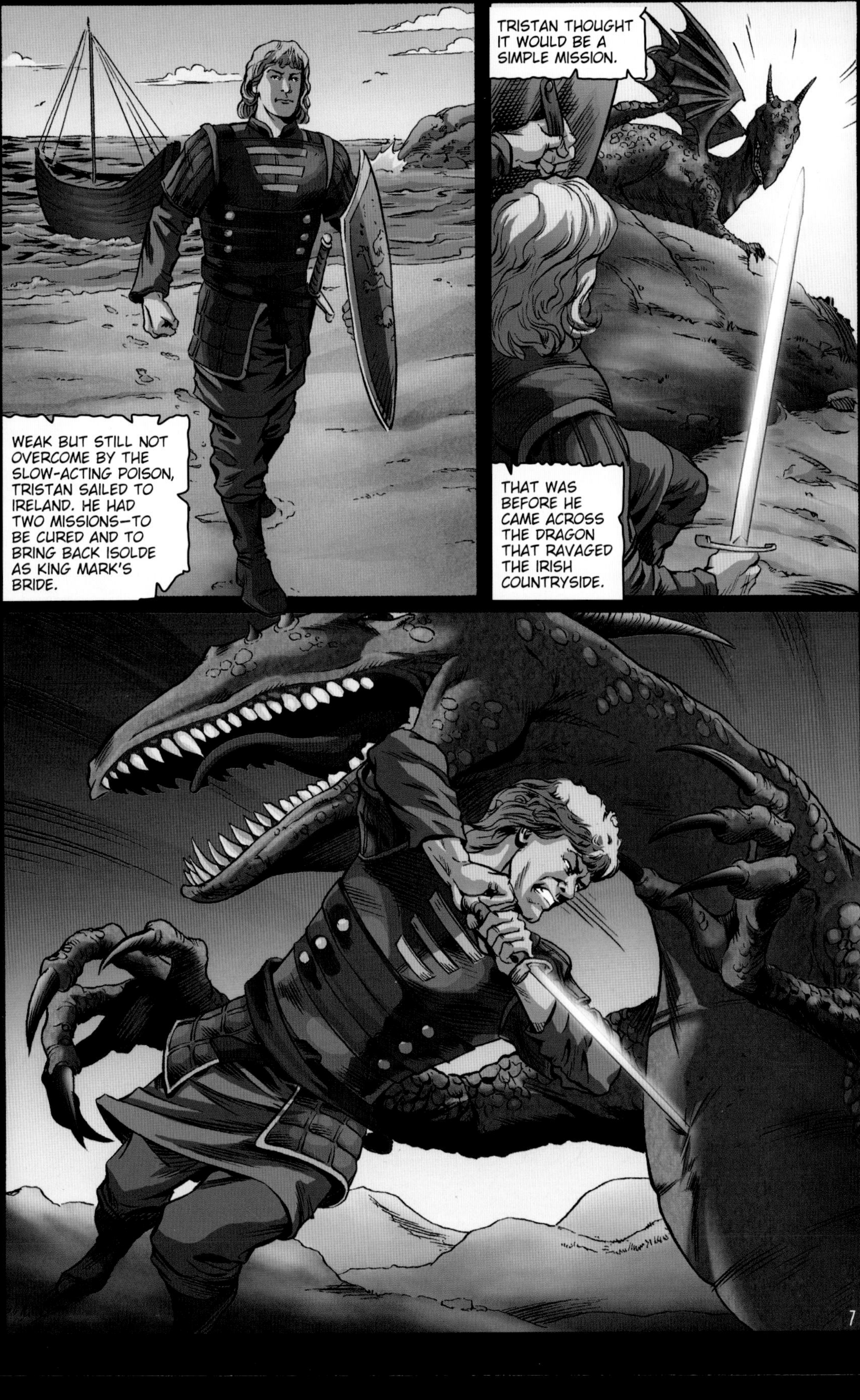
WEAK BUT STILL NOT OVERCOME BY THE SLOW-ACTING POISON, TRISTAN SAILED TO IRELAND. HE HAD TWO MISSIONS—TO BE CURED AND TO BRING BACK ISOLDE AS KING MARK'S BRIDE.
TRISTAN THOUGHT IT WOULD BE A SIMPLE MISSION.
THAT WAS BEFORE HE CAME ACROSS THE DRAGON THAT RAVAGED THE IRISH COUNTRYSIDE.

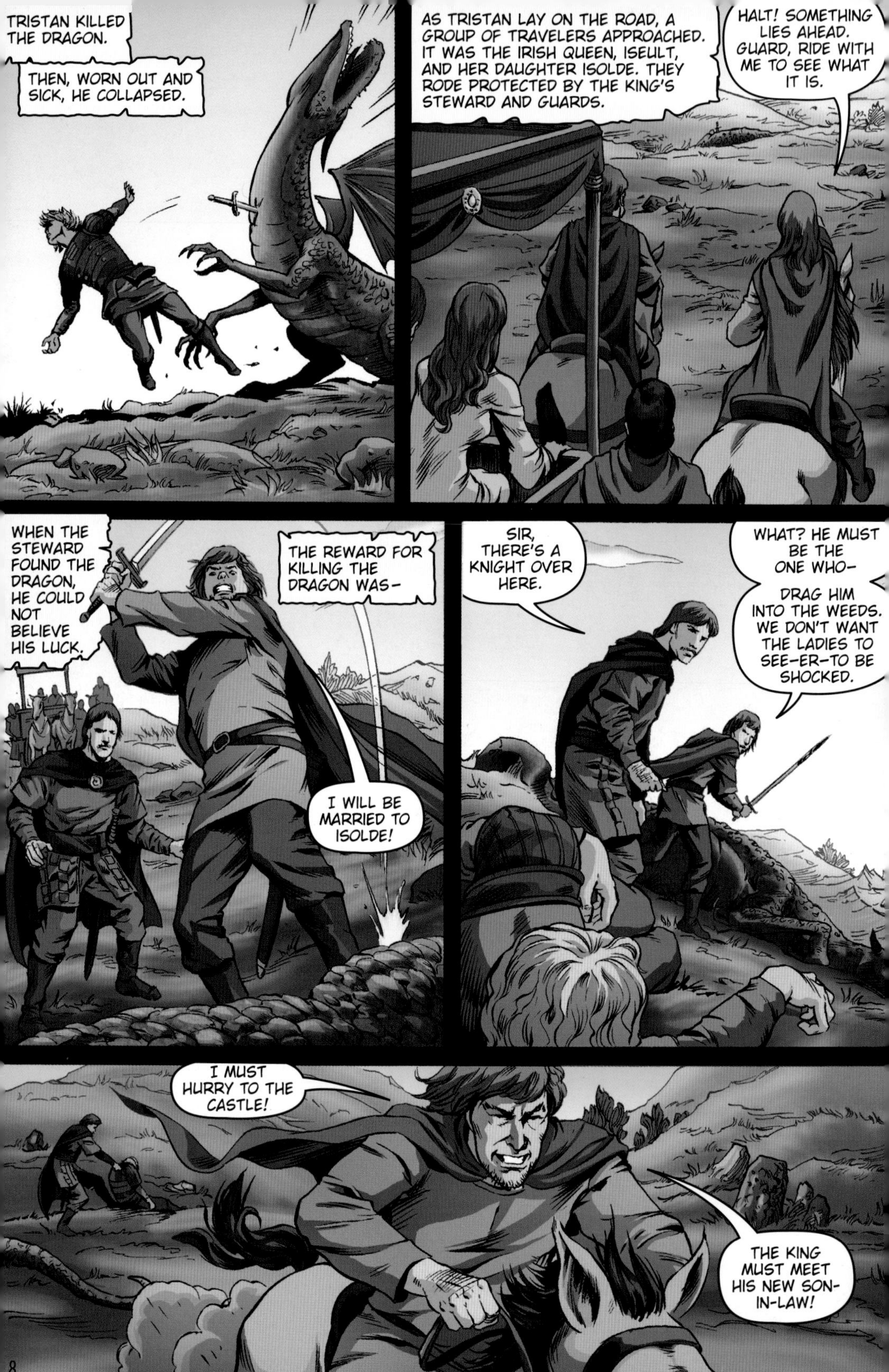
TRISTAN KILLED THE DRAGON.
THEN, WORN OUT AND SICK, HE COLLAPSED.
AS TRISTAN LAY ON THE ROAD, A GROUP OF TRAVELERS APPROACHED. IT WAS THE IRISH QUEEN, ISEULT, AND HER DAUGHTER ISOLDE. THEY RODE PROTECTED BY THE KING'S STEWARD AND GUARDS.
HALT! SOMETHING LIES AHEAD. GUARD, RIDE WITH ME TO SEE WHAT IT IS.
WHEN THE STEWARD FOUND THE DRAGON, HE COULD NOT BELIEVE HIS LUCK.
THE REWARD FOR KILLING THE DRAGON WAS-
I WILL BE MARRIED TO ISOLDE!
SIR, THERE'S A KNIGHT OVER HERE.
WHAT? HE MUST BE THE ONE WHO-
DRAG HIM INTO THE WEEDS. WE DON'T WANT THE LADIES TO SEE-ER-TO BE SHOCKED.
I MUST HURRY TO THE CASTLE!
THE KING MUST MEET HIS NEW SON-IN-LAW!

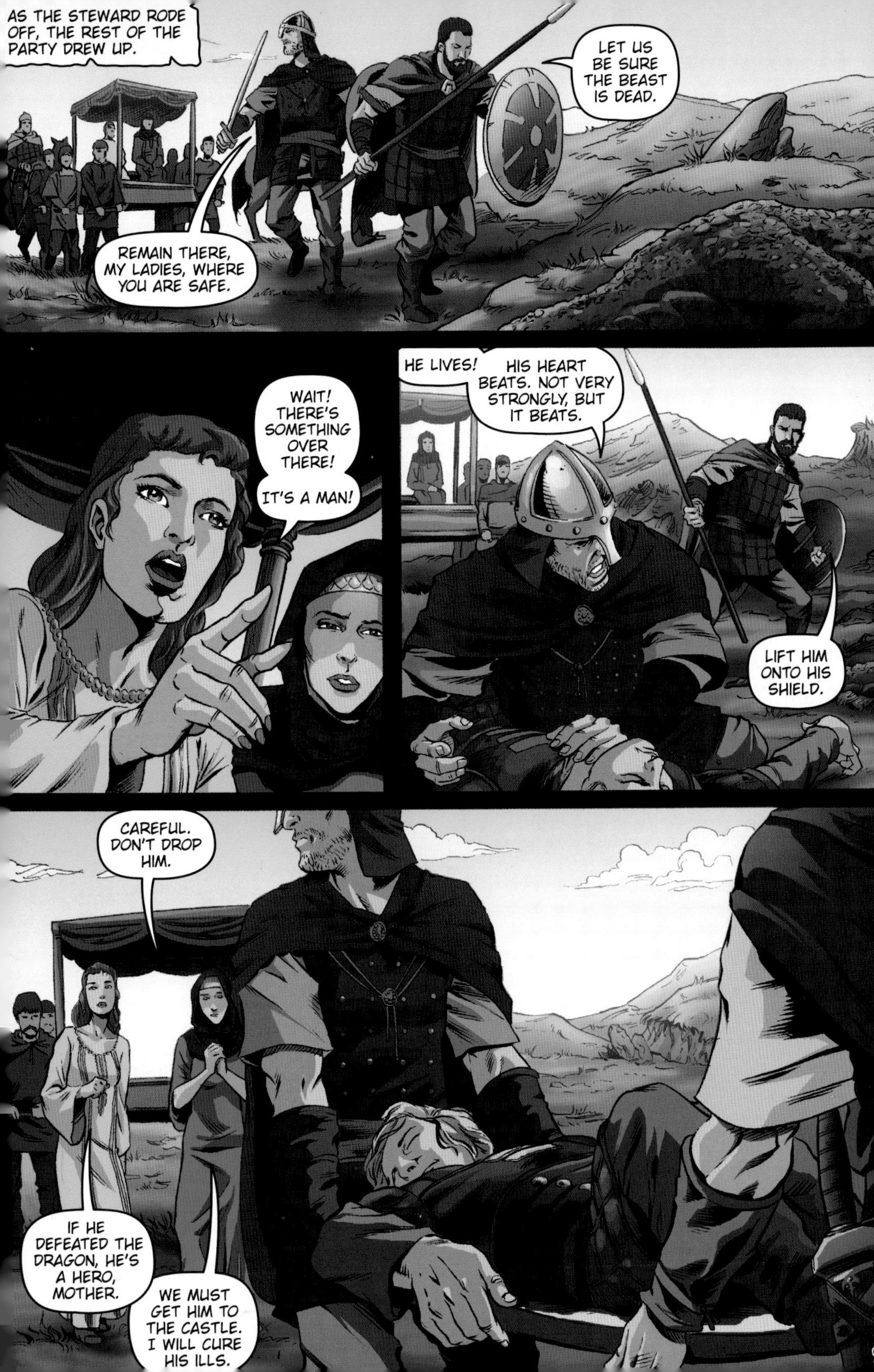
AS THE STEWARD RODE OFF, THE REST OF THE PARTY DREW UP.
LET US BE SURE THE BEAST IS DEAD.
REMAIN THERE, MY LADIES, WHERE YOU ARE SAFE.
WAIT! THERE'S SOMETHING OVER THERE!
IT'S A MAN!
HE LIVES!
HIS HEART BEATS. NOT VERY STRONGLY, BUT IT BEATS.
LIFT HIM ONTO HIS SHIELD.
CAREFUL. DON'T DROP HIM.
IF HE DEFEATED THE DRAGON, HE'S A HERO, MOTHER.
WE MUST GET HIM TO THE CASTLE. I WILL CURE HIS ILLS.

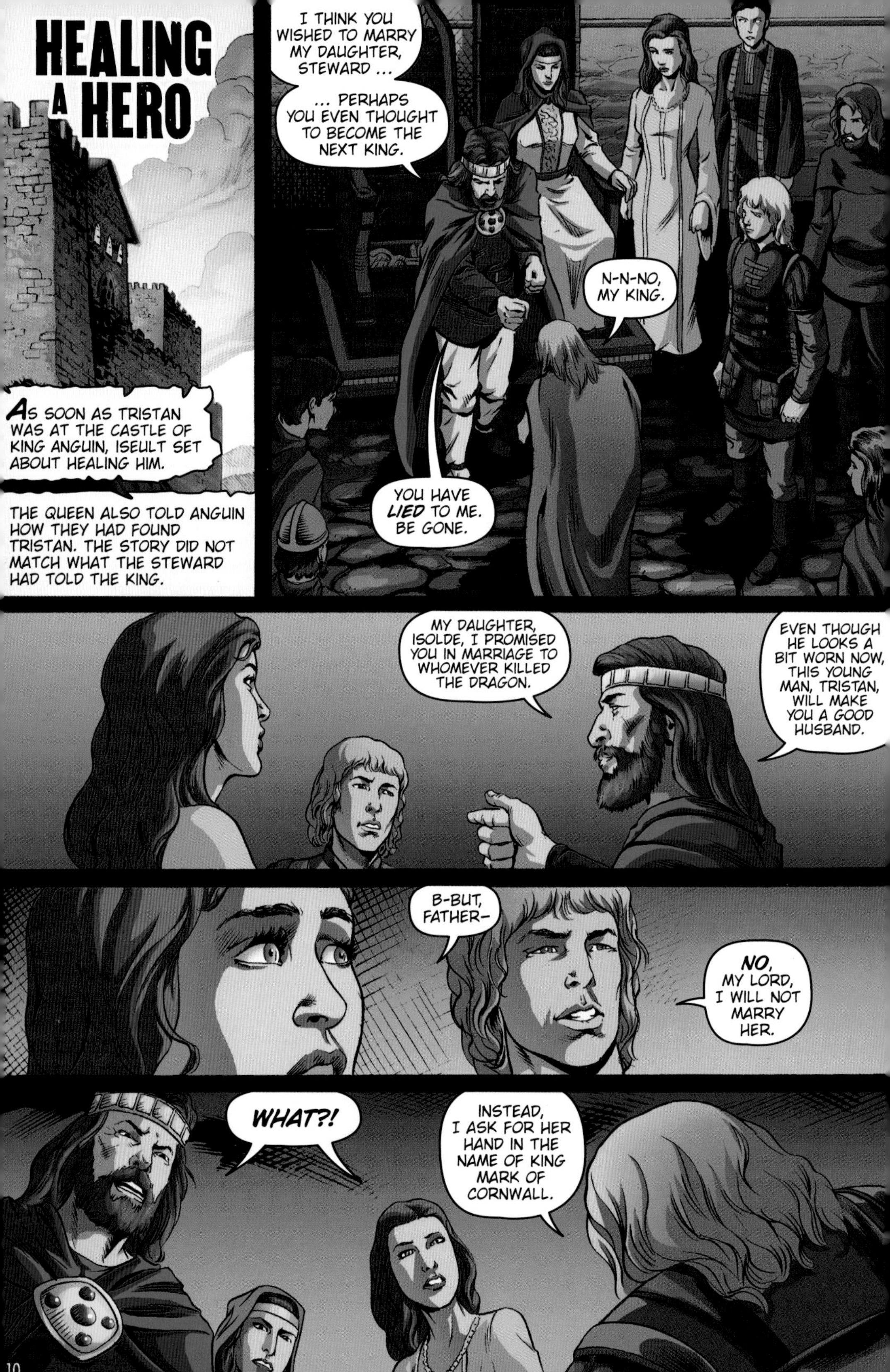

HEALING A HERO
AS SOON AS TRISTAN WAS AT THE CASTLE OF KING ANGUIN, ISEULT SET ABOUT HEALING HIM.
THE QUEEN ALSO TOLD ANGUIN HOW THEY HAD FOUND TRISTAN. THE STORY DID NOT MATCH WHAT THE STEWARD HAD TOLD THE KING.
I THINK YOU WISHED TO MARRY MY DAUGHTER, STEWARD ...
... PERHAPS YOU EVEN THOUGHT TO BECOME THE NEXT KING.
N-N-NO, MY KING.
YOU HAVE LIED TO ME. BE GONE.
MY DAUGHTER, ISOLDE, I PROMISED YOU IN MARRIAGE TO WHOMEVER KILLED THE DRAGON.
EVEN THOUGH HE LOOKS A BIT WORN NOW, THIS YOUNG MAN, TRISTAN, WILL MAKE YOU A GOOD HUSBAND.
B-BUT, FATHER-
NO, MY LORD, I WILL NOT MARRY HER.
WHAT?!
INSTEAD, I ASK FOR HER HAND IN THE NAME OF KING MARK OF CORNWALL.

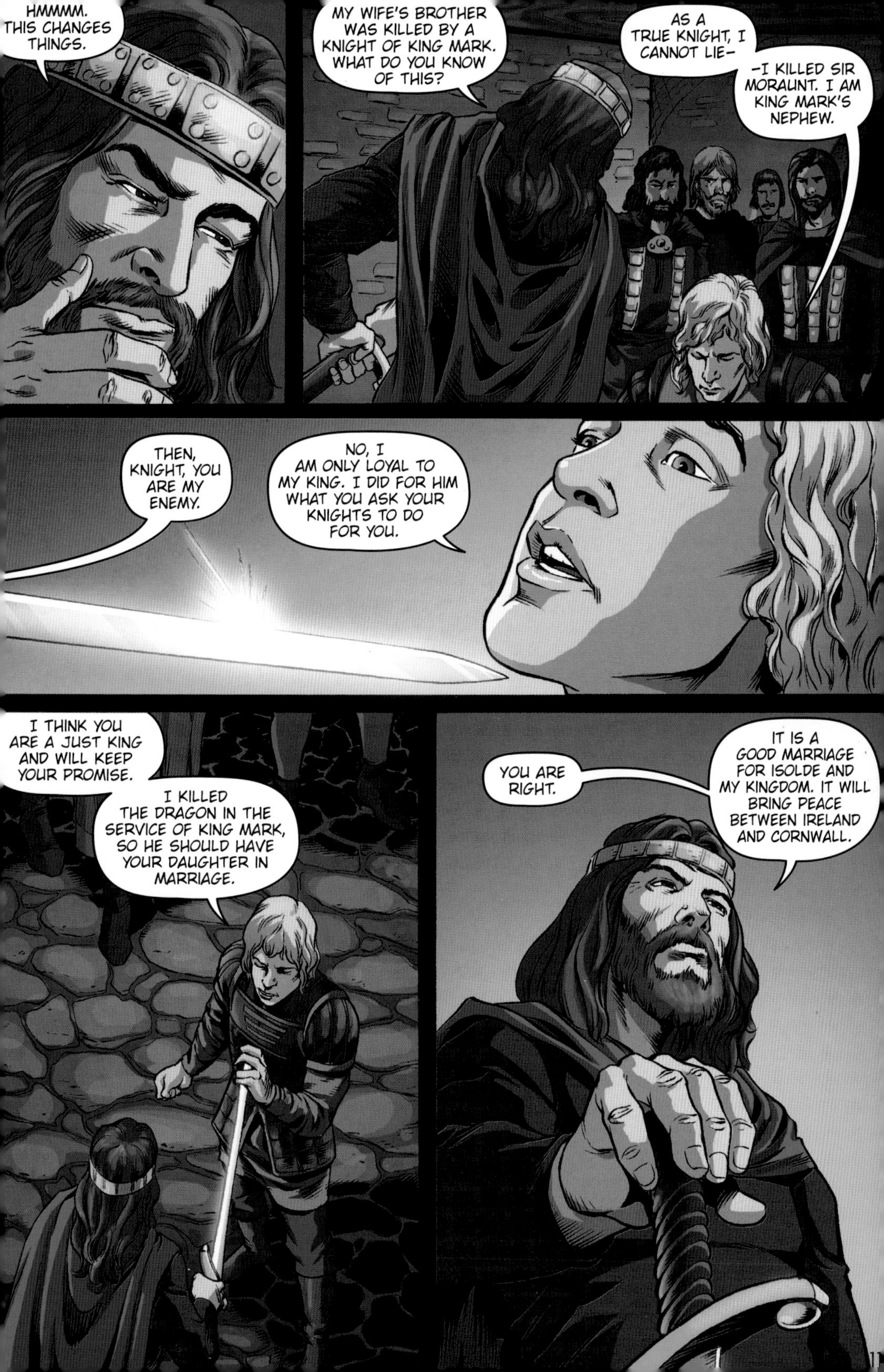
HMMMM. THIS CHANGES THINGS.
MY WIFE'S BROTHER WAS KILLED BY A KNIGHT OF KING MARK. WHAT DO YOU KNOW OF THIS?
AS A TRUE KNIGHT, I CANNOT LIE-
-I KILLED SIR MORAUNT. I AM KING MARK'S NEPHEW.
THEN, KNIGHT, YOU ARE MY ENEMY.
NO, I AM ONLY LOYAL TO MY KING. I DID FOR HIM WHAT YOU ASK YOUR KNIGHTS TO DO FOR YOU.
I THINK YOU ARE A JUST KING AND WILL KEEP YOUR PROMISE.
I KILLED THE DRAGON IN THE SERVICE OF KING MARK, SO HE SHOULD HAVE YOUR DAUGHTER IN MARRIAGE.
YOU ARE RIGHT.
IT IS A GOOD MARRIAGE FOR ISOLDE AND MY KINGDOM. IT WILL BRING PEACE BETWEEN IRELAND AND CORNWALL.

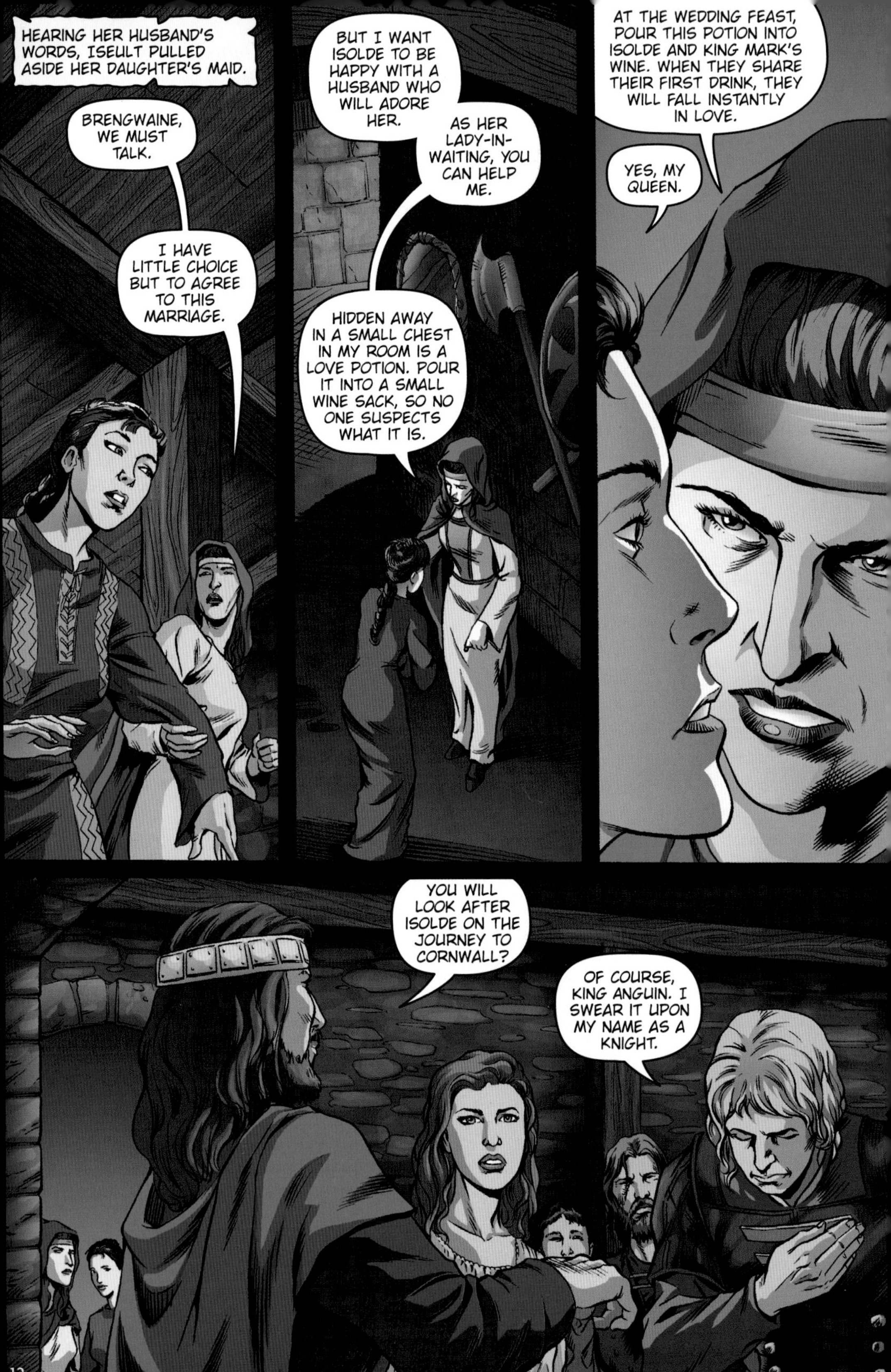
HEARING HER HUSBAND'S WORDS, ISEULT PULLED ASIDE HER DAUGHTER'S MAID.
BRENGWAINE, WE MUST TALK.
I HAVE LITTLE CHOICE BUT TO AGREE TO THIS MARRIAGE.
BUT I WANT ISOLDE TO BE HAPPY WITH A HUSBAND WHO WILL ADORE HER.
AS HER LADY-IN-WAITING, YOU CAN HELP ME.
HIDDEN AWAY IN A SMALL CHEST IN MY ROOM IS A LOVE POTION. POUR IT INTO A SMALL WINE SACK, SO NO ONE SUSPECTS WHAT IT IS.
AT THE WEDDING FEAST, POUR THIS POTION INTO ISOLDE AND KING MARK'S WINE. WHEN THEY SHARE THEIR FIRST DRINK, THEY WILL FALL INSTANTLY IN LOVE.
YES, MY QUEEN.
YOU WILL LOOK AFTER ISOLDE ON THE JOURNEY TO CORNWALL?
OF COURSE, KING ANGUIN. I SWEAR IT UPON MY NAME AS A KNIGHT.

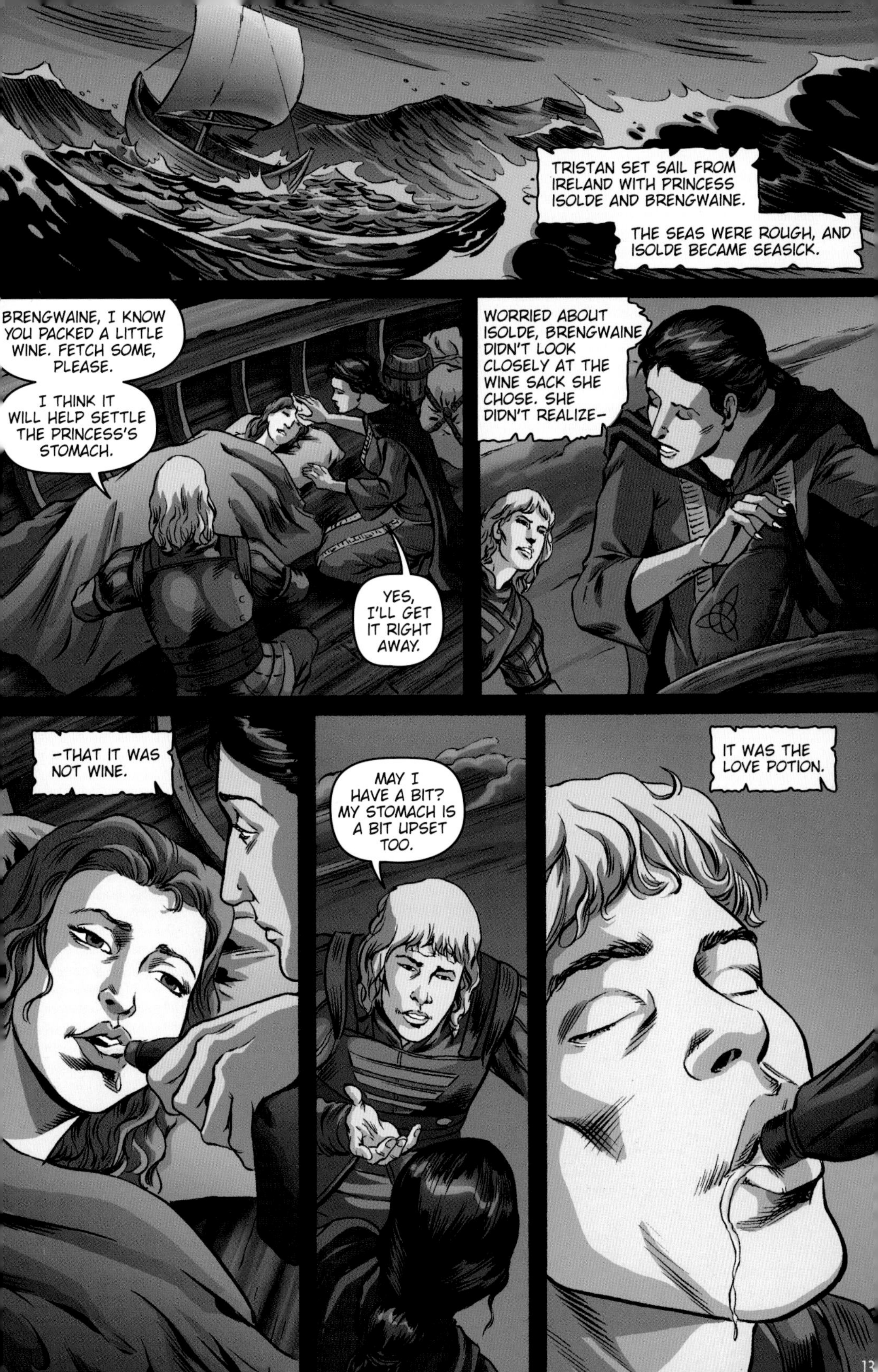
TRISTAN SET SAIL FROM IRELAND WITH PRINCESS ISOLDE AND BRENGWAINE.
THE SEAS WERE ROUGH, AND ISOLDE BECAME SEASICK.
BRENGWAINE, I KNOW YOU PACKED A LITTLE WINE. FETCH SOME, PLEASE.
I THINK IT WILL HELP SETTLE THE PRINCESS'S STOMACH.
YES, I'LL GET IT RIGHT AWAY.
WORRIED ABOUT ISOLDE, BRENGWAINE DIDN'T LOOK CLOSELY AT THE WINE SACK SHE CHOSE. SHE DIDN'T REALIZE–
–THAT IT WAS NOT WINE.
MAY I HAVE A BIT? MY STOMACH IS A BIT UPSET TOO.
IT WAS THE LOVE POTION.

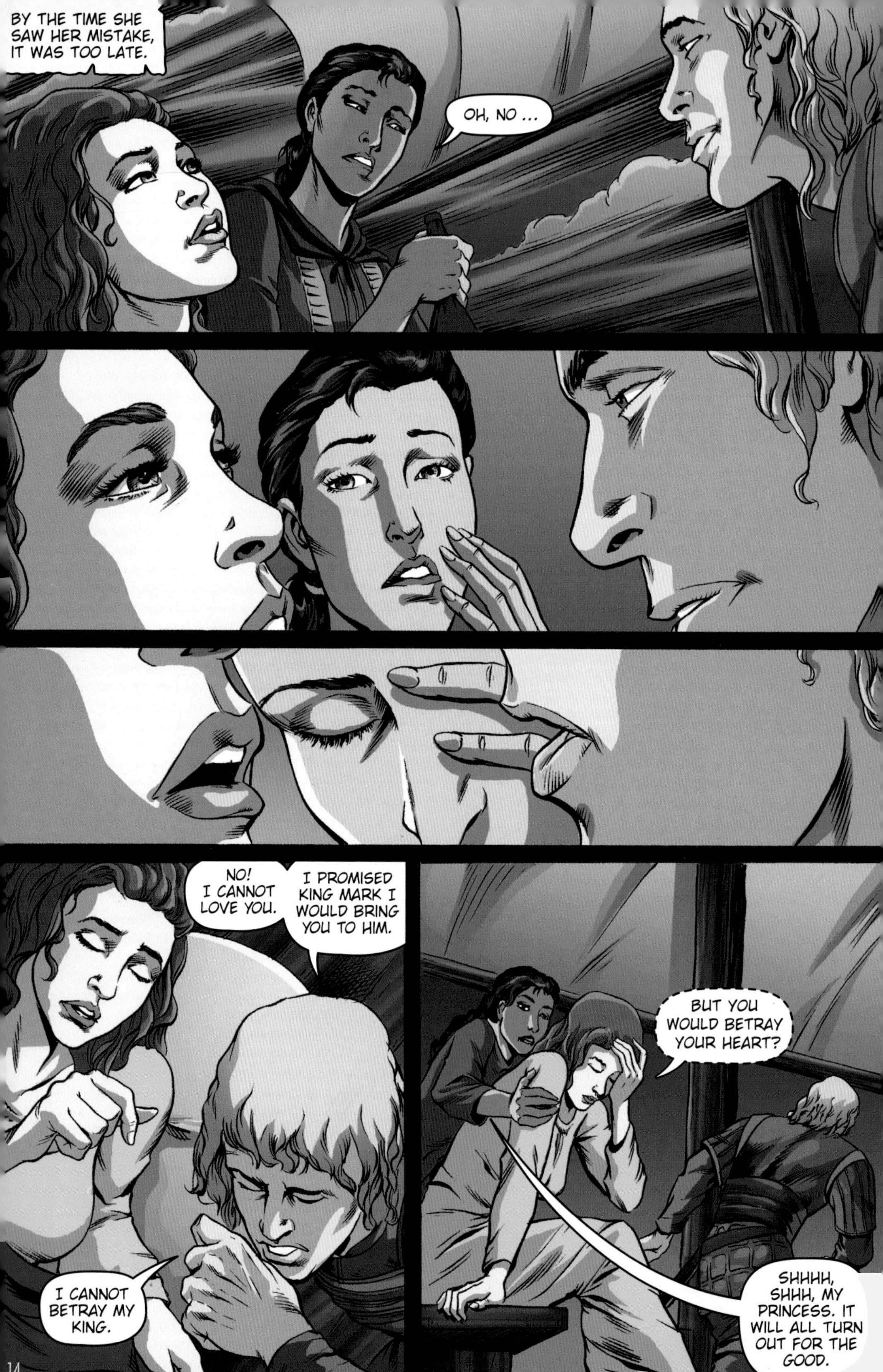
BY THE TIME SHE SAW HER MISTAKE, IT WAS TOO LATE.
OH, NO ...
NO! I CANNOT LOVE YOU.
I PROMISED KING MARK I WOULD BRING YOU TO HIM.
I CANNOT BETRAY MY KING.
BUT YOU WOULD BETRAY YOUR HEART?
SHHHH, SHHH, MY PRINCESS. IT WILL ALL TURN OUT FOR THE GOOD.

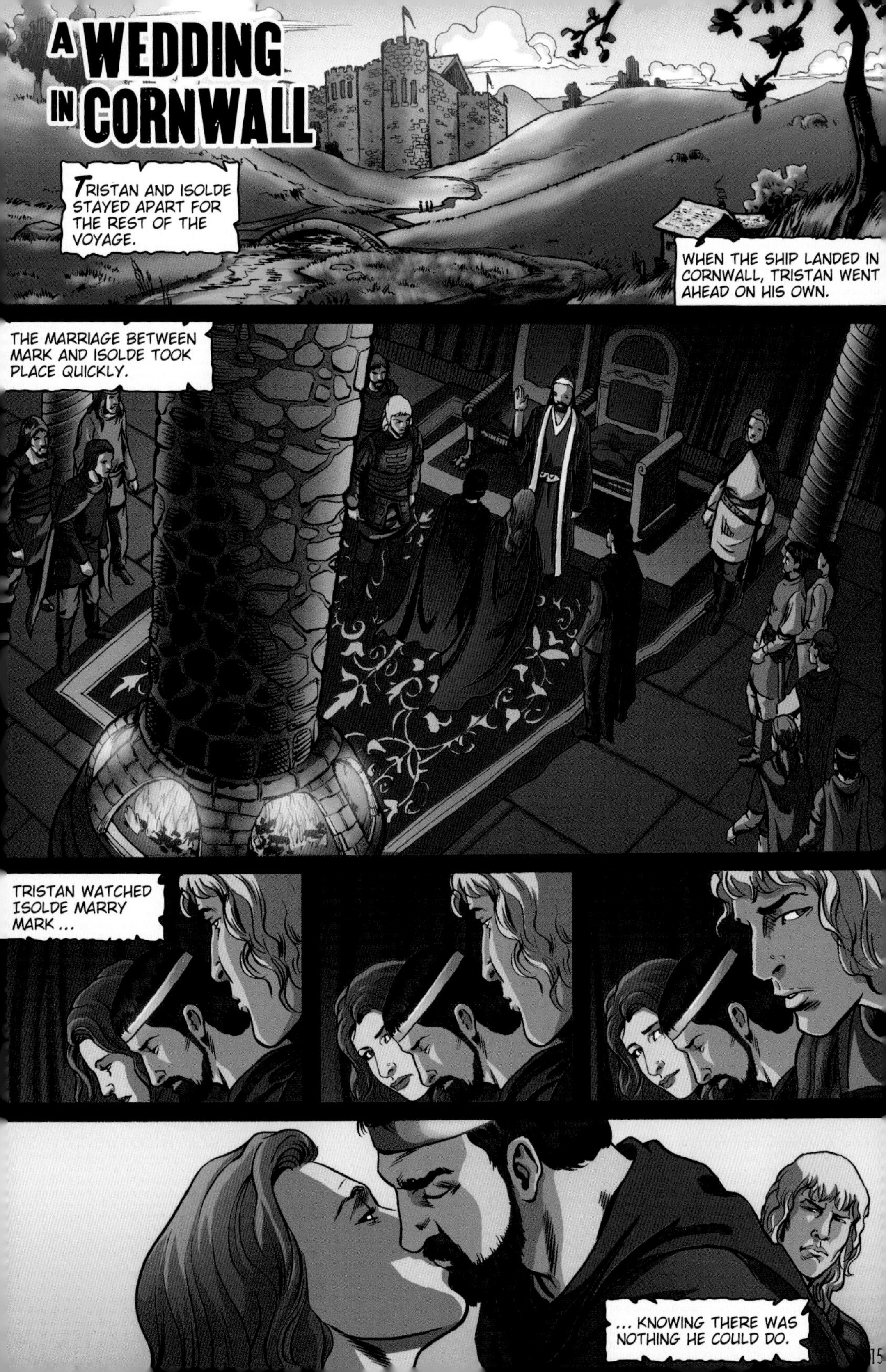
A WEDDING IN CORNWALL
TRISTAN AND ISOLDE STAYED APART FOR THE REST OF THE VOYAGE.
WHEN THE SHIP LANDED IN CORNWALL, TRISTAN WENT AHEAD ON HIS OWN.
THE MARRIAGE BETWEEN MARK AND ISOLDE TOOK PLACE QUICKLY.
TRISTAN WATCHED ISOLDE MARRY MARK ...
... KNOWING THERE WAS NOTHING HE COULD DO.

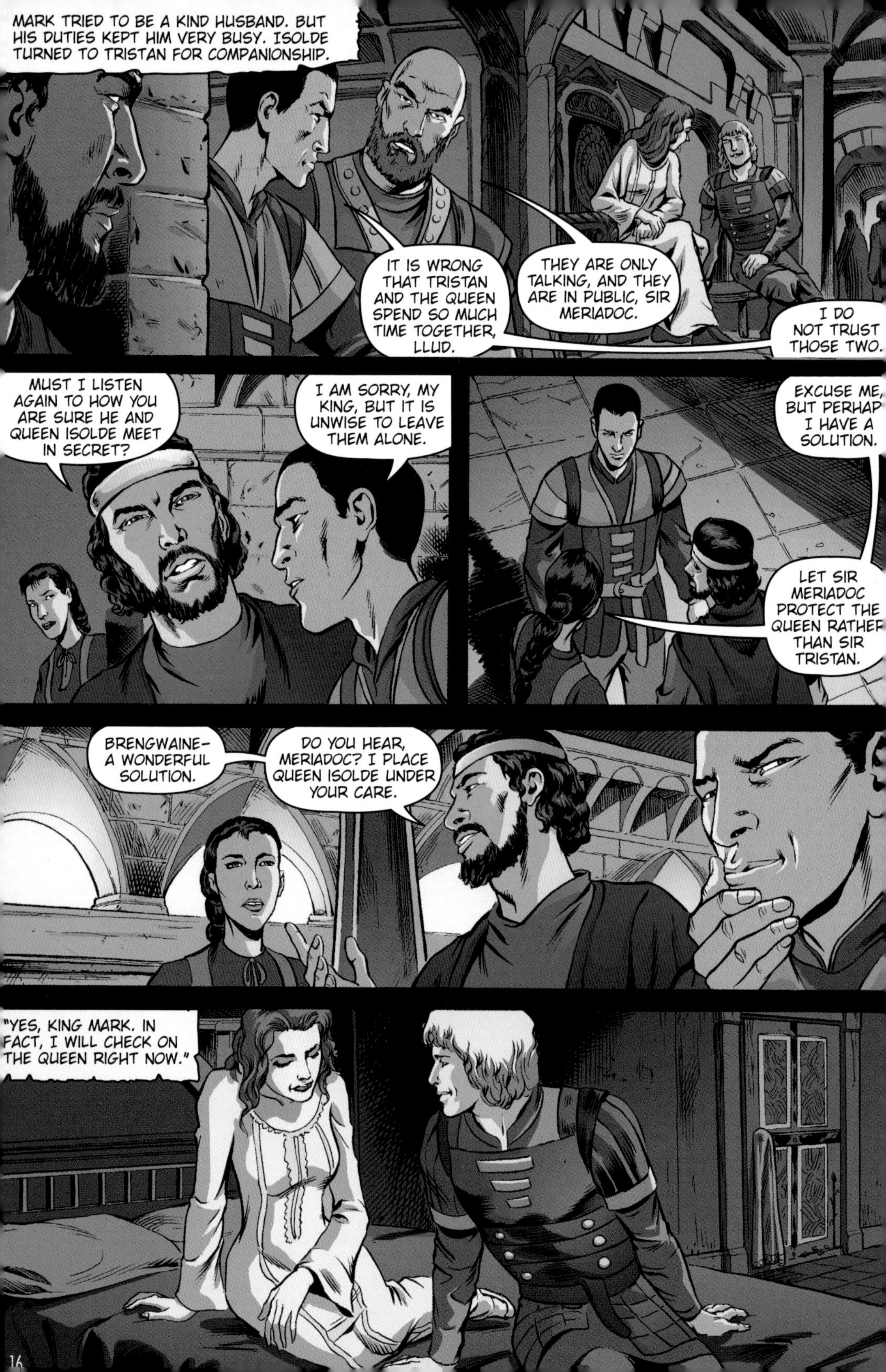
MARK TRIED TO BE A KIND HUSBAND. BUT HIS DUTIES KEPT HIM VERY BUSY. ISOLDE TURNED TO TRISTAN FOR COMPANIONSHIP.
IT IS WRONG THAT TRISTAN AND THE QUEEN SPEND SO MUCH TIME TOGETHER, LLUD.
THEY ARE ONLY TALKING, AND THEY ARE IN PUBLIC, SIR MERIADOC.
I DO NOT TRUST THOSE TWO.
MUST I LISTEN AGAIN TO HOW YOU ARE SURE HE AND QUEEN ISOLDE MEET IN SECRET?
I AM SORRY, MY KING, BUT IT IS UNWISE TO LEAVE THEM ALONE.
EXCUSE ME, BUT PERHAP I HAVE A SOLUTION.
LET SIR MERIADOC PROTECT THE QUEEN RATHER THAN SIR TRISTAN.
BRENGWAINE— A WONDERFUL SOLUTION.
DO YOU HEAR, MERIADOC? I PLACE QUEEN ISOLDE UNDER YOUR CARE.
"YES, KING MARK. IN FACT, I WILL CHECK ON THE QUEEN RIGHT NOW."

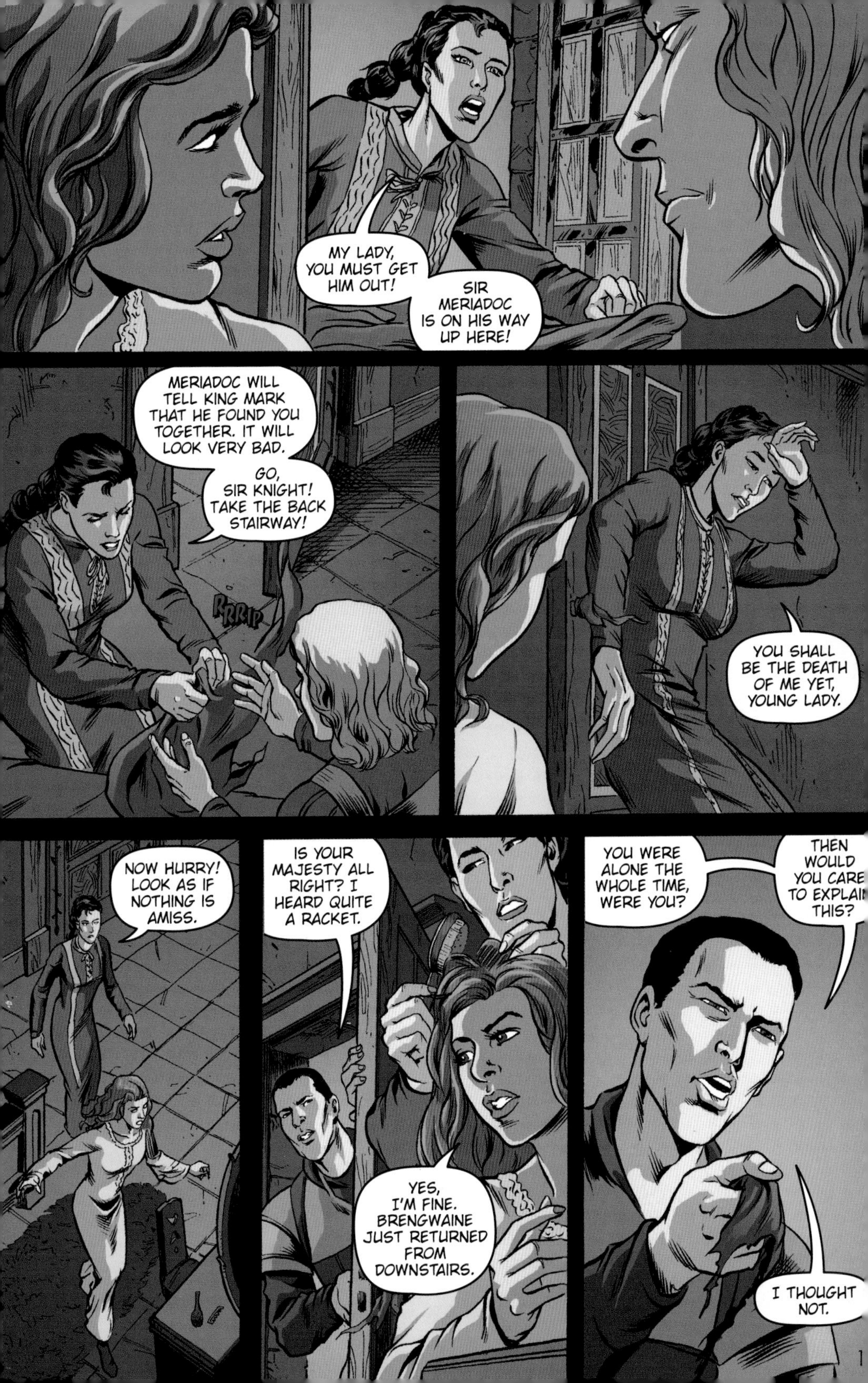
MY LADY, YOU MUST GET HIM OUT!
SIR MERIADOC IS ON HIS WAY UP HERE!
MERIADOC WILL TELL KING MARK THAT HE FOUND YOU TOGETHER. IT WILL LOOK VERY BAD.
GO, SIR KNIGHT! TAKE THE BACK STAIRWAY!
RRRIP
YOU SHALL BE THE DEATH OF ME YET, YOUNG LADY.
NOW HURRY! LOOK AS IF NOTHING IS AMISS.
IS YOUR MAJESTY ALL RIGHT? I HEARD QUITE A RACKET.
YES, I'M FINE. BRENGWAINE JUST RETURNED FROM DOWNSTAIRS.
YOU WERE ALONE THE WHOLE TIME, WERE YOU?
THEN WOULD YOU CARE TO EXPLAIN THIS?
I THOUGHT NOT.

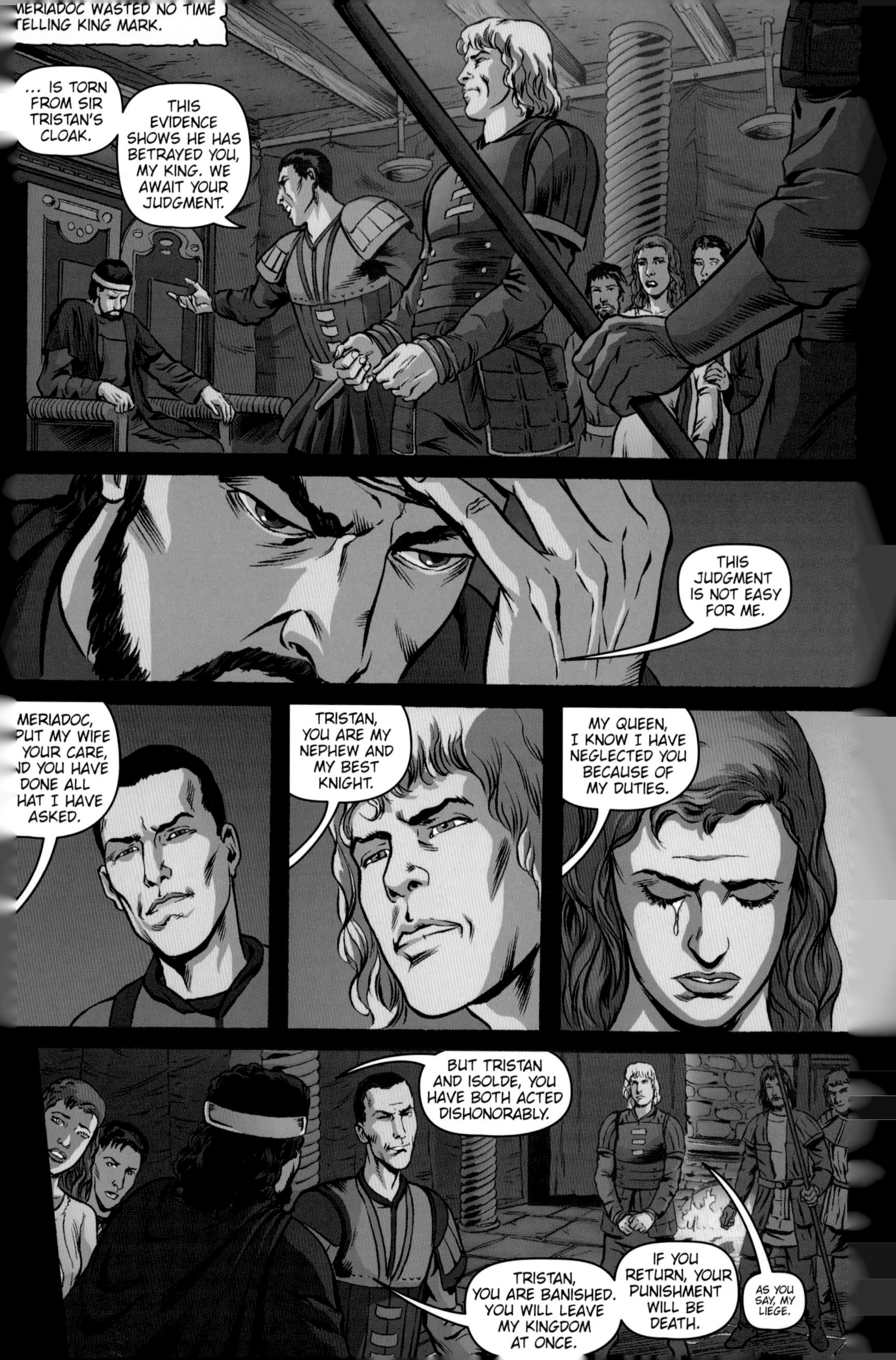
MERIADOC WASTED NO TIME TELLING KING MARK.
... IS TORN FROM SIR TRISTAN'S CLOAK.
THIS EVIDENCE SHOWS HE HAS BETRAYED YOU, MY KING. WE AWAIT YOUR JUDGMENT.
THIS JUDGMENT IS NOT EASY FOR ME.
MERIADOC, PUT MY WIFE YOUR CARE, ND YOU HAVE DONE ALL HAT I HAVE ASKED.
TRISTAN, YOU ARE MY NEPHEW AND MY BEST KNIGHT.
MY QUEEN, I KNOW I HAVE NEGLECTED YOU BECAUSE OF MY DUTIES.
BUT TRISTAN AND ISOLDE, YOU HAVE BOTH ACTED DISHONORABLY.
TRISTAN, YOU ARE BANISHED. YOU WILL LEAVE MY KINGDOM AT ONCE.
IF YOU RETURN, YOUR PUNISHMENT WILL BE DEATH.
AS YOU SAY, MY LIEGE.

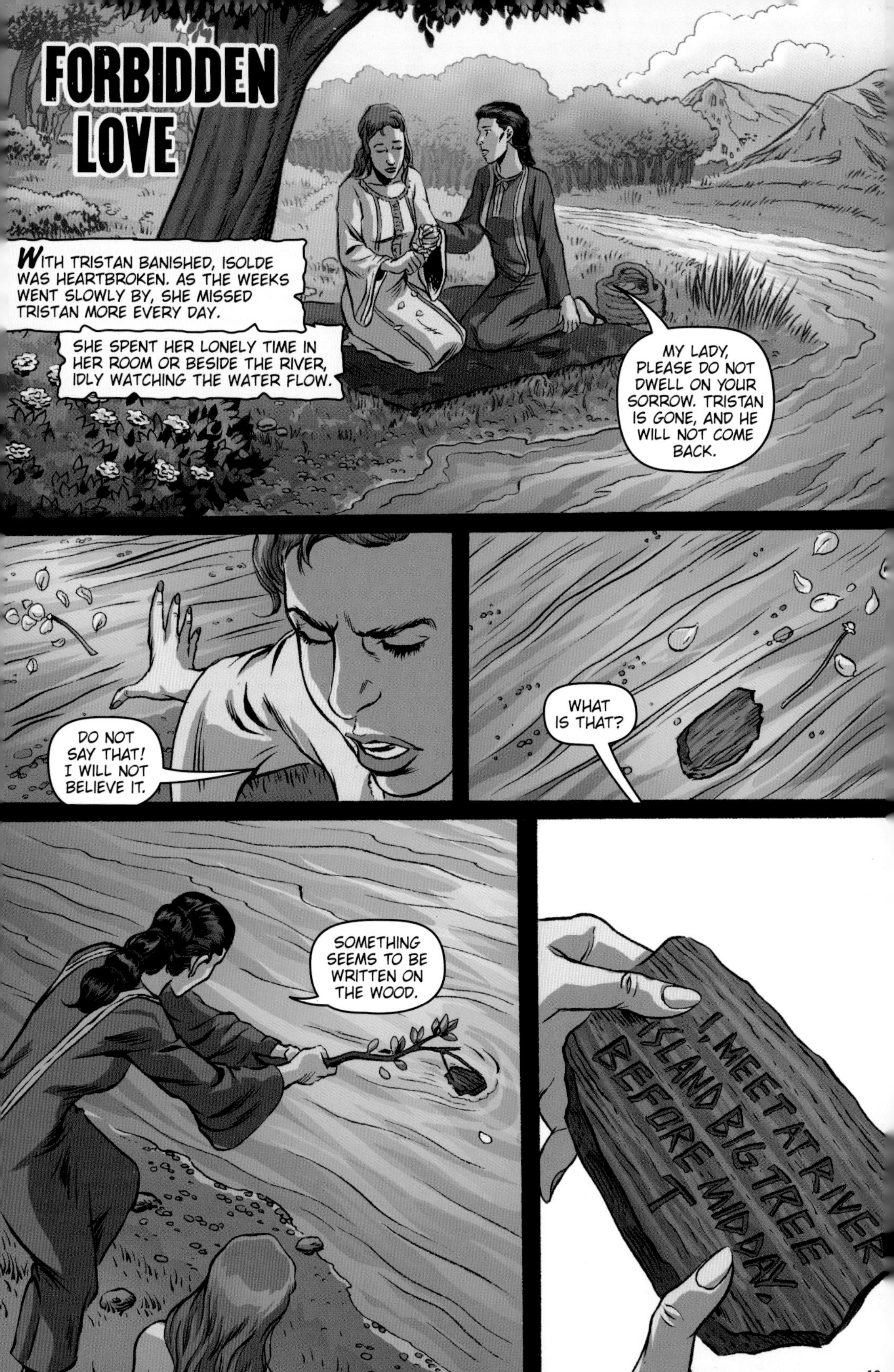
FORBIDDEN LOVE
WITH TRISTAN BANISHED, ISOLDE WAS HEARTBROKEN. AS THE WEEKS WENT SLOWLY BY, SHE MISSED TRISTAN MORE EVERY DAY.
SHE SPENT HER LONELY TIME IN HER ROOM OR BESIDE THE RIVER, IDLY WATCHING THE WATER FLOW.
MY LADY, PLEASE DO NOT DWELL ON YOUR SORROW. TRISTAN IS GONE, AND HE WILL NOT COME BACK.
DO NOT SAY THAT! I WILL NOT BELIEVE IT.
WHAT IS THAT?
SOMETHING SEEMS TO BE WRITTEN ON THE WOOD.
I. MEET AT RIVER ISLAND BIG TREE BEFORE MIDDAY. T

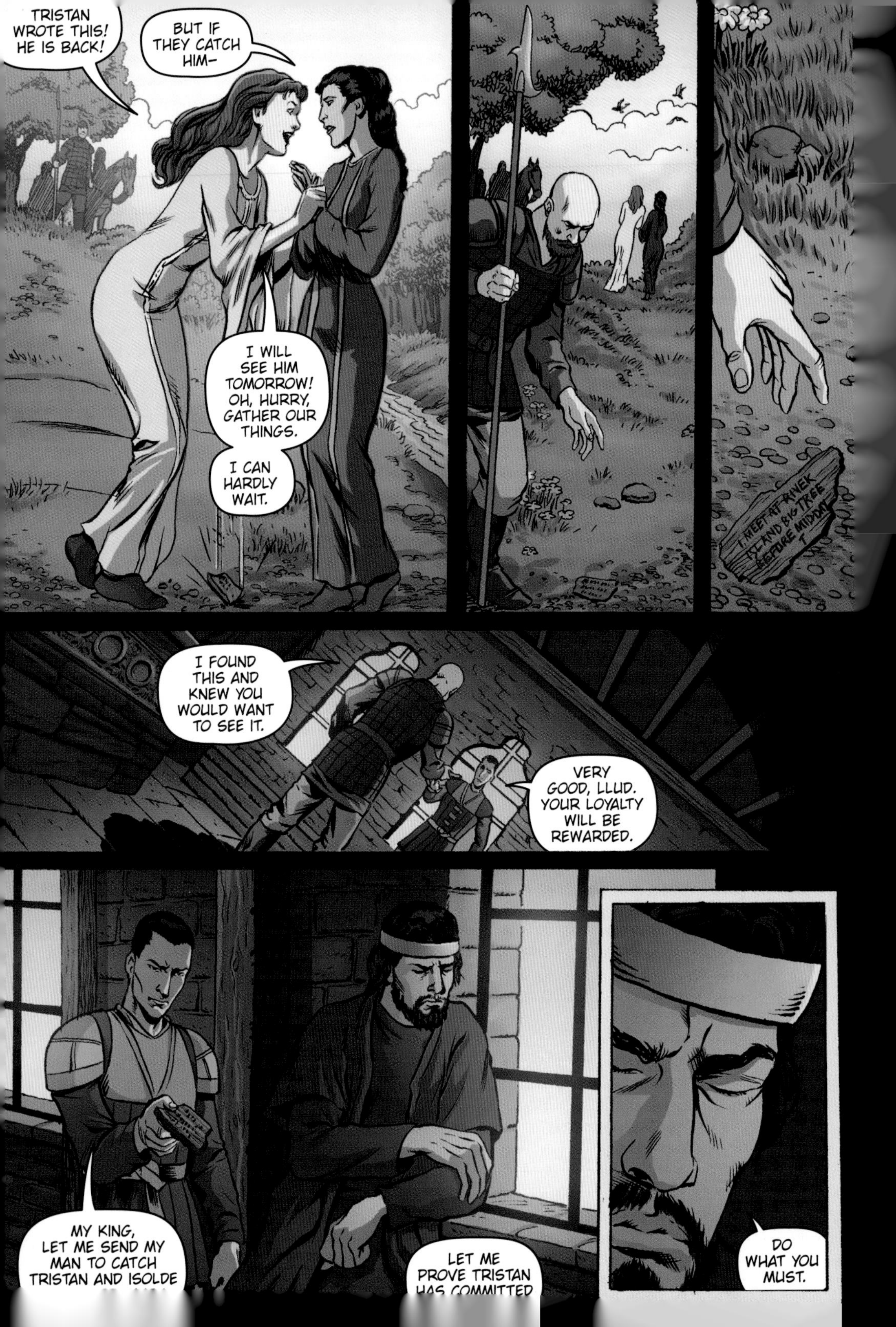

TRISTAN WROTE THIS! HE IS BACK!
BUT IF THEY CATCH HIM-
I WILL SEE HIM TOMORROW! OH, HURRY, GATHER OUR THINGS.
I CAN HARDLY WAIT.
I MEET AT RIVER ISLAND BIG TREE BEFORE MIDDAY T
I FOUND THIS AND KNEW YOU WOULD WANT TO SEE IT.
VERY GOOD, LLUD. YOUR LOYALTY WILL BE REWARDED.
MY KING, LET ME SEND MY MAN TO CATCH TRISTAN AND ISOLDE
LET ME PROVE TRISTAN HAS COMMITTED
DO WHAT YOU MUST.

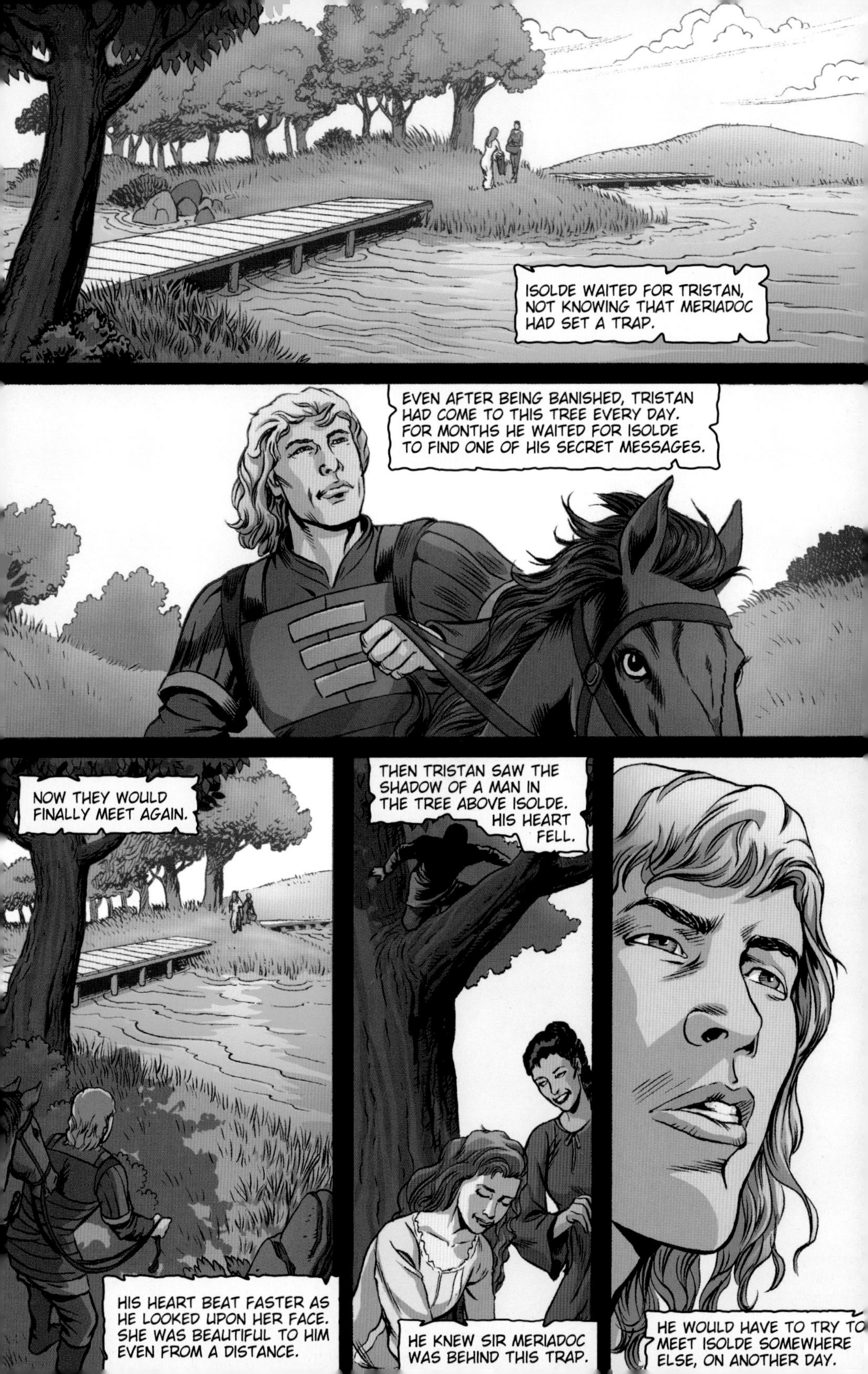
ISOLDE WAITED FOR TRISTAN, NOT KNOWING THAT MERIADOC HAD SET A TRAP.
EVEN AFTER BEING BANISHED, TRISTAN HAD COME TO THIS TREE EVERY DAY. FOR MONTHS HE WAITED FOR ISOLDE TO FIND ONE OF HIS SECRET MESSAGES.
NOW THEY WOULD FINALLY MEET AGAIN.
HIS HEART BEAT FASTER AS HE LOOKED UPON HER FACE. SHE WAS BEAUTIFUL TO HIM EVEN FROM A DISTANCE.
THEN TRISTAN SAW THE SHADOW OF A MAN IN THE TREE ABOVE ISOLDE. HIS HEART FELL.
HE KNEW SIR MERIADOC WAS BEHIND THIS TRAP.
HE WOULD HAVE TO TRY TO MEET ISOLDE SOMEWHERE ELSE, ON ANOTHER DAY.

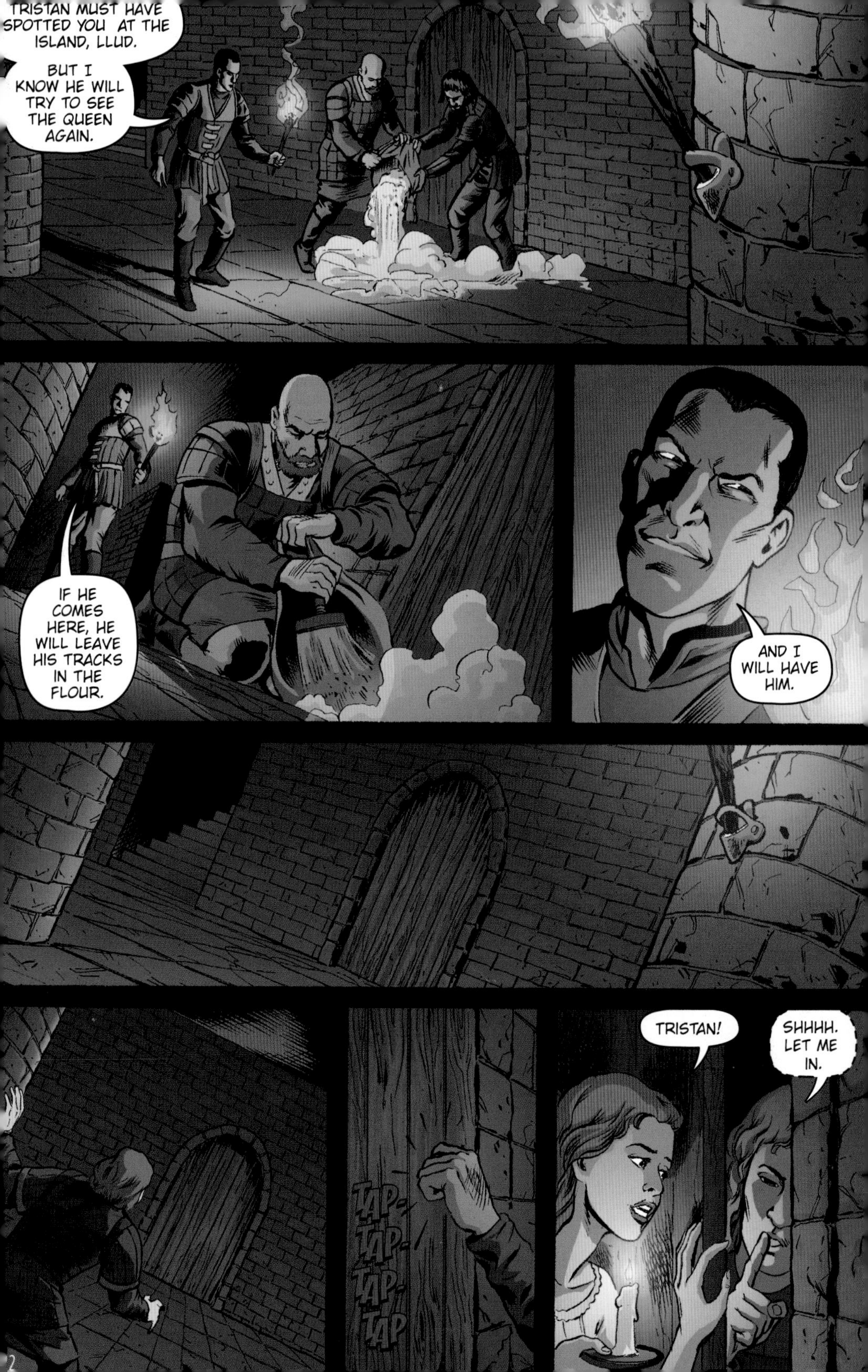
TRISTAN MUST HAVE SPOTTED YOU AT THE ISLAND, LLUD.
BUT I KNOW HE WILL TRY TO SEE THE QUEEN AGAIN.
IF HE COMES HERE, HE WILL LEAVE HIS TRACKS IN THE FLOUR.
AND I WILL HAVE HIM.
TAP-TAP-TAP-TAP
TRISTAN!
SHHHH. LET ME IN.

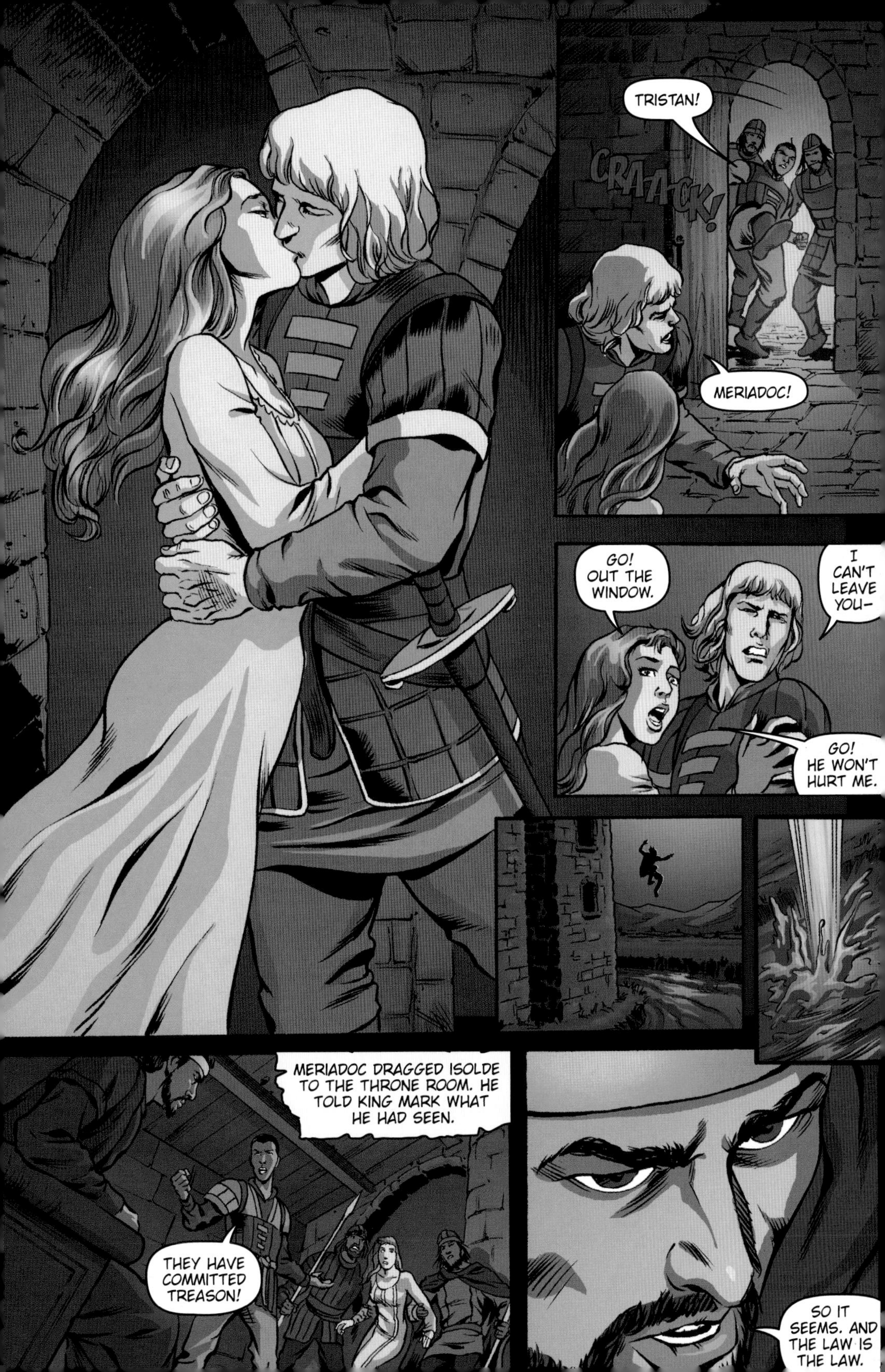
TRISTAN!
CRAAACK!
MERIADOC!
GO! OUT THE WINDOW.
I CAN'T LEAVE YOU—
GO! HE WON'T HURT ME.
MERIADOC DRAGGED ISOLDE TO THE THRONE ROOM. HE TOLD KING MARK WHAT HE HAD SEEN.
THEY HAVE COMMITTED TREASON!
SO IT SEEMS. AND THE LAW IS THE LAW.

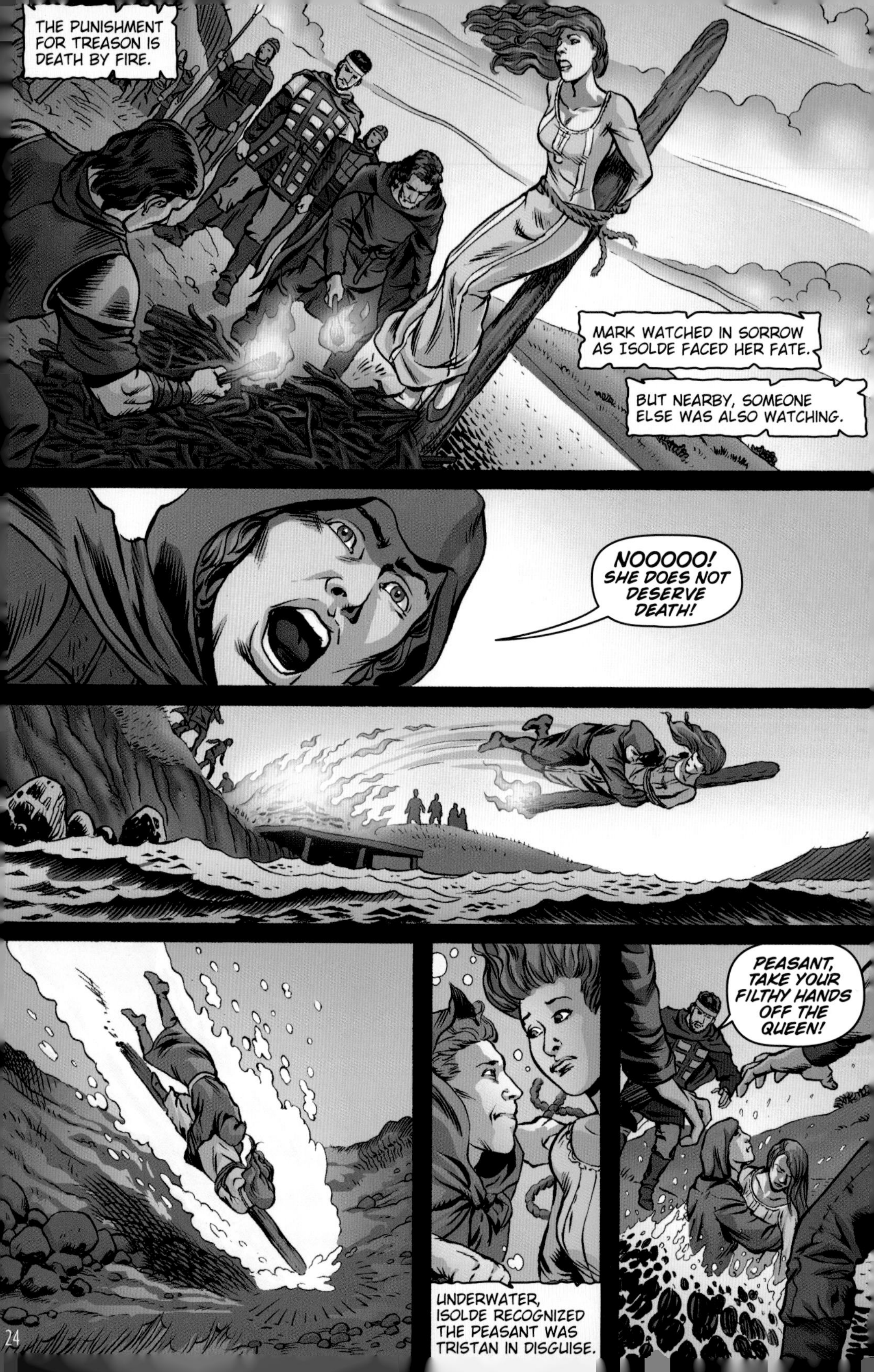
THE PUNISHMENT FOR TREASON IS DEATH BY FIRE.
MARK WATCHED IN SORROW AS ISOLDE FACED HER FATE.
BUT NEARBY, SOMEONE ELSE WAS ALSO WATCHING.
NOOOOO! SHE DOES NOT DESERVE DEATH!
UNDERWATER, ISOLDE RECOGNIZED THE PEASANT WAS TRISTAN IN DISGUISE.
PEASANT, TAKE YOUR FILTHY HANDS OFF THE QUEEN!

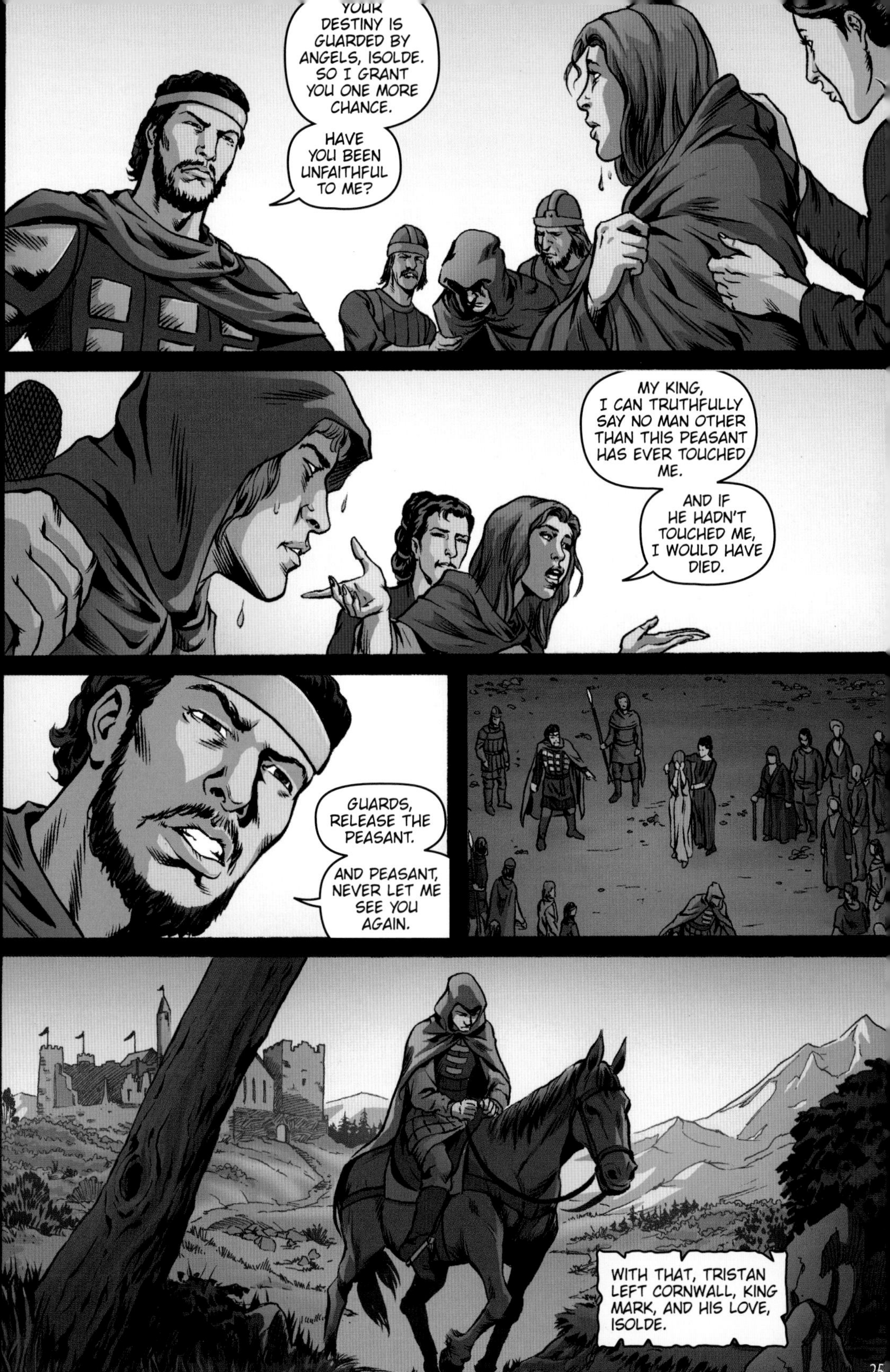
YOUR DESTINY IS GUARDED BY ANGELS, ISOLDE. SO I GRANT YOU ONE MORE CHANCE.
HAVE YOU BEEN UNFAITHFUL TO ME?
MY KING, I CAN TRUTHFULLY SAY NO MAN OTHER THAN THIS PEASANT HAS EVER TOUCHED ME.
AND IF HE HADN'T TOUCHED ME, I WOULD HAVE DIED.
GUARDS, RELEASE THE PEASANT.
AND PEASANT, NEVER LET ME SEE YOU AGAIN.
WITH THAT, TRISTAN LEFT CORNWALL, KING MARK, AND HIS LOVE, ISOLDE.

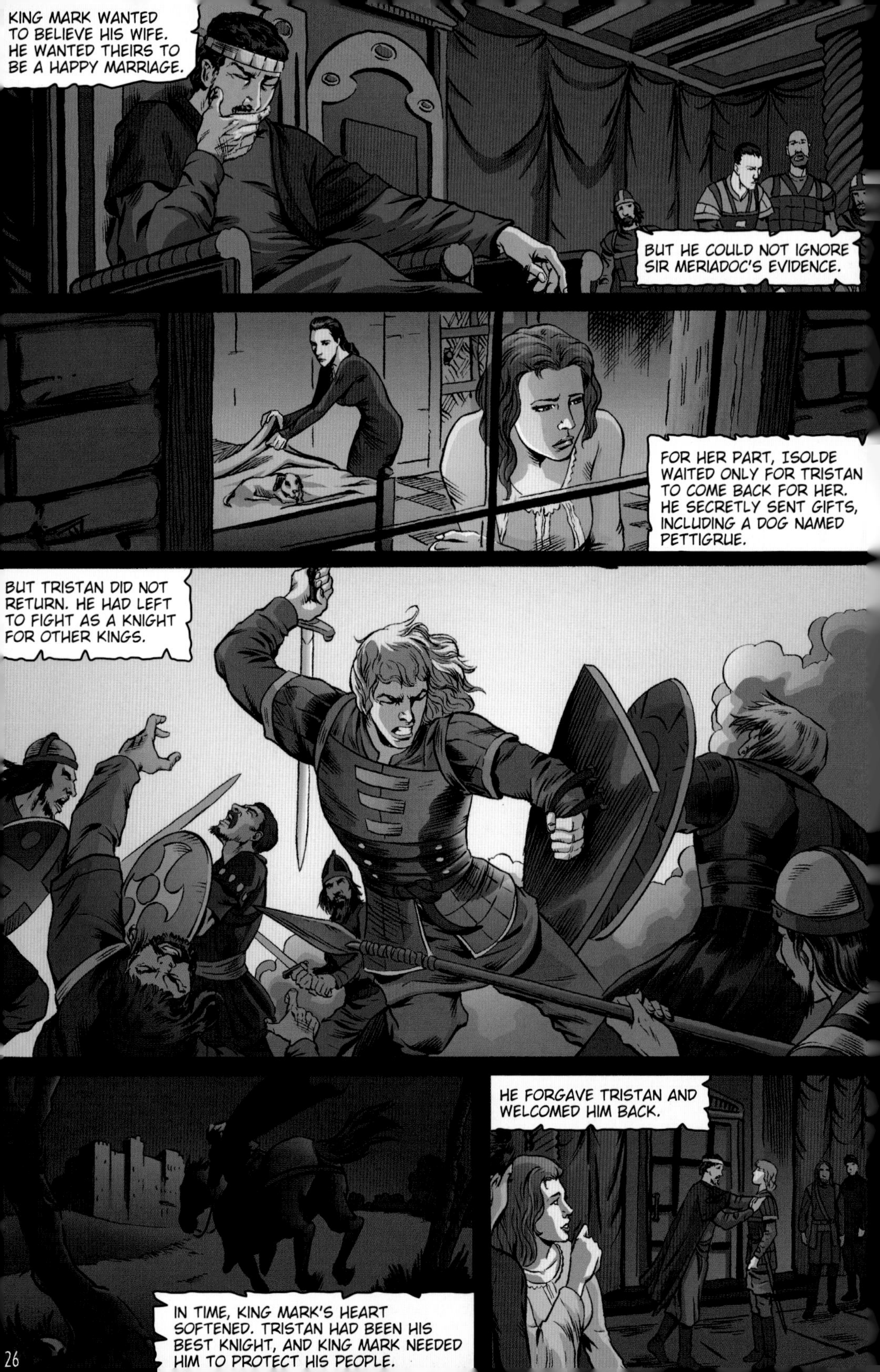
KING MARK WANTED TO BELIEVE HIS WIFE. HE WANTED THEIRS TO BE A HAPPY MARRIAGE.
BUT HE COULD NOT IGNORE SIR MERIADOC'S EVIDENCE.
FOR HER PART, ISOLDE WAITED ONLY FOR TRISTAN TO COME BACK FOR HER. HE SECRETLY SENT GIFTS, INCLUDING A DOG NAMED PETTIGRUE.
BUT TRISTAN DID NOT RETURN. HE HAD LEFT TO FIGHT AS A KNIGHT FOR OTHER KINGS.
IN TIME, KING MARK'S HEART SOFTENED. TRISTAN HAD BEEN HIS BEST KNIGHT, AND KING MARK NEEDED HIM TO PROTECT HIS PEOPLE.
HE FORGAVE TRISTAN AND WELCOMED HIM BACK.

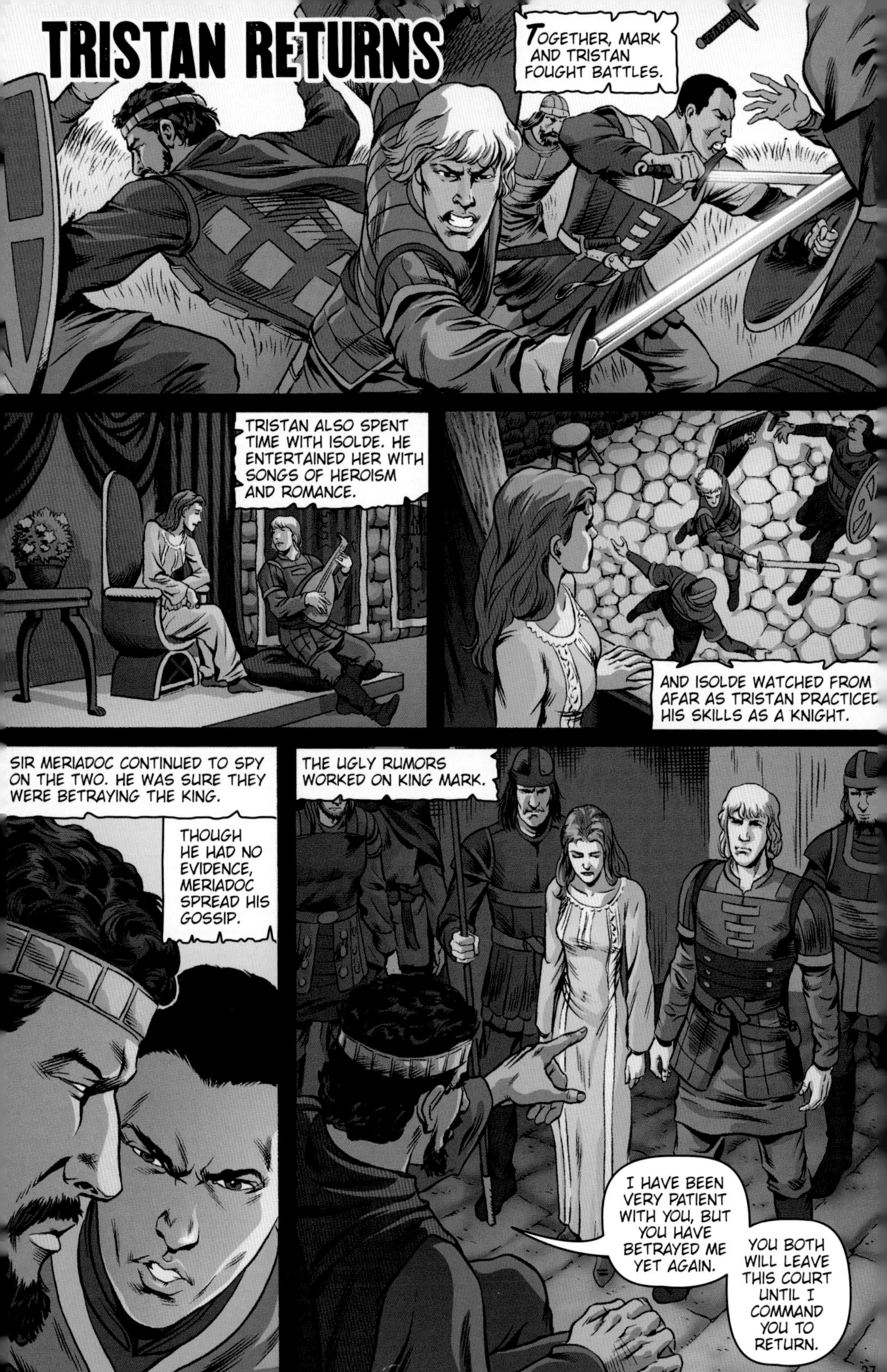
TRISTAN RETURNS
TOGETHER, MARK AND TRISTAN FOUGHT BATTLES.
TRISTAN ALSO SPENT TIME WITH ISOLDE. HE ENTERTAINED HER WITH SONGS OF HEROISM AND ROMANCE.
AND ISOLDE WATCHED FROM AFAR AS TRISTAN PRACTICED HIS SKILLS AS A KNIGHT.
SIR MERIADOC CONTINUED TO SPY ON THE TWO. HE WAS SURE THEY WERE BETRAYING THE KING.
THOUGH HE HAD NO EVIDENCE, MERIADOC SPREAD HIS GOSSIP.
THE UGLY RUMORS WORKED ON KING MARK.
I HAVE BEEN VERY PATIENT WITH YOU, BUT YOU HAVE BETRAYED ME YET AGAIN.
YOU BOTH WILL LEAVE THIS COURT UNTIL I COMMAND YOU TO RETURN.

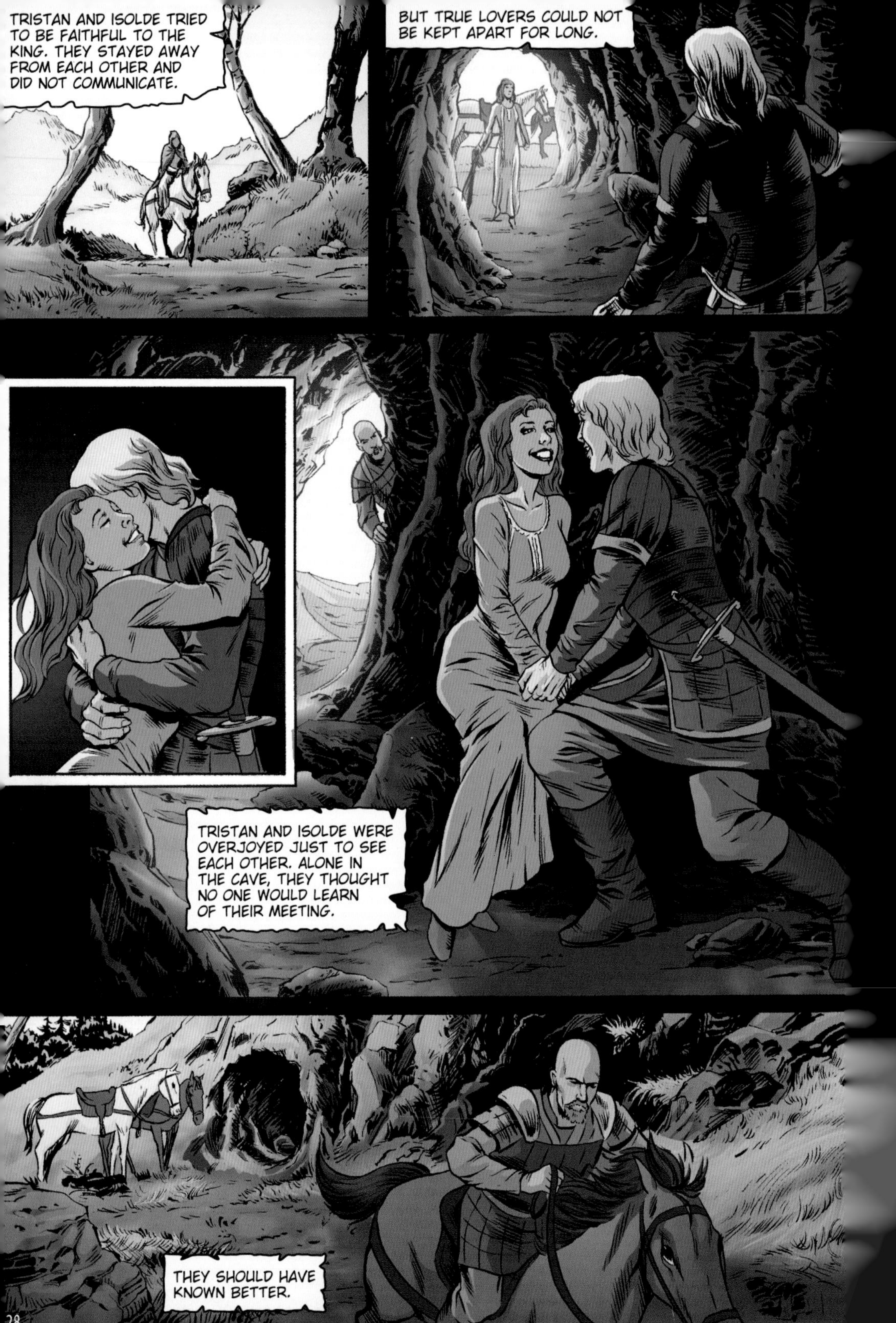
TRISTAN AND ISOLDE TRIED TO BE FAITHFUL TO THE KING. THEY STAYED AWAY FROM EACH OTHER AND DID NOT COMMUNICATE.
BUT TRUE LOVERS COULD NOT BE KEPT APART FOR LONG.
TRISTAN AND ISOLDE WERE OVERJOYED JUST TO SEE EACH OTHER. ALONE IN THE CAVE, THEY THOUGHT NO ONE WOULD LEARN OF THEIR MEETING.
THEY SHOULD HAVE KNOWN BETTER.

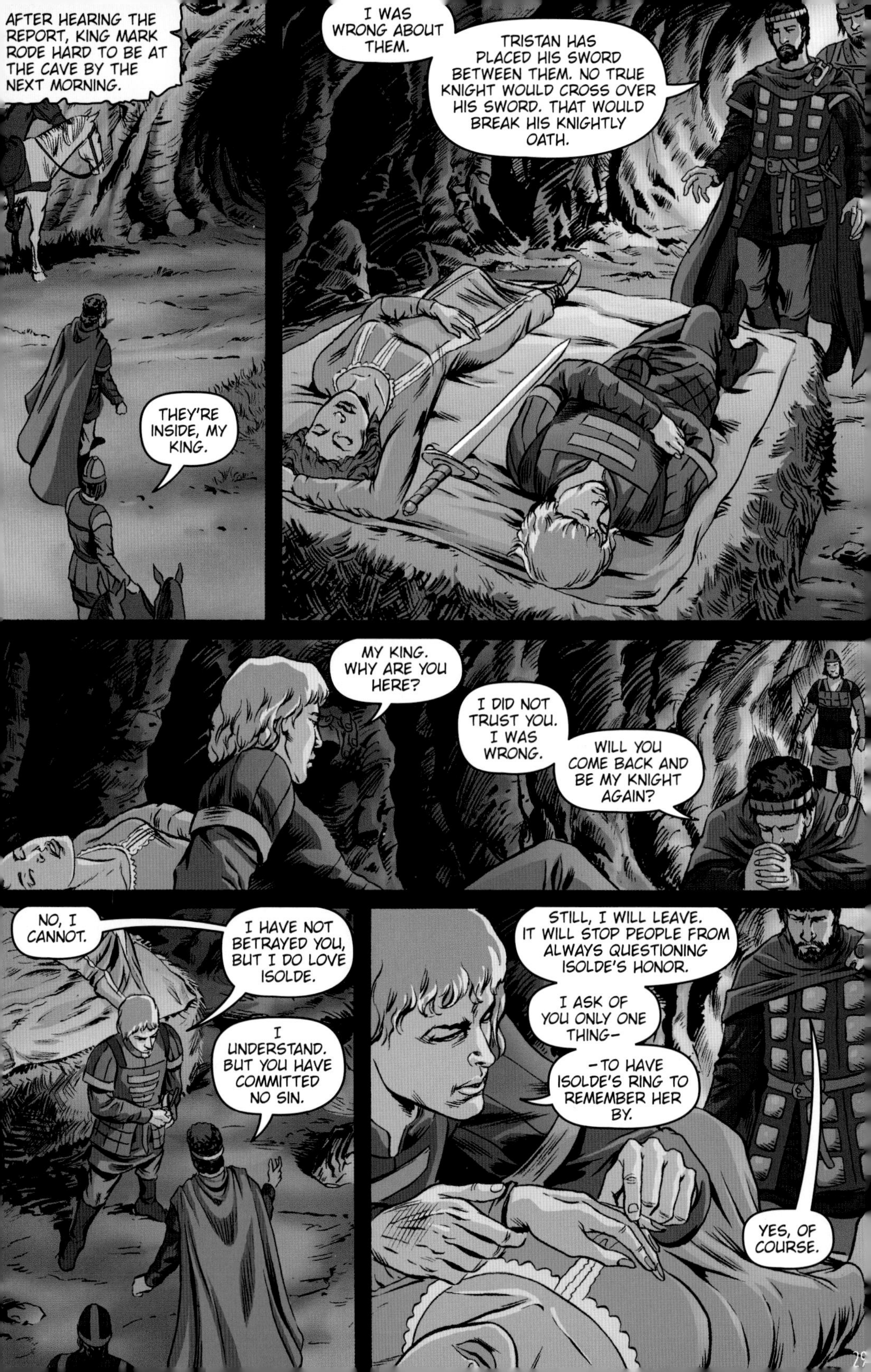
AFTER HEARING THE REPORT, KING MARK RODE HARD TO BE AT THE CAVE BY THE NEXT MORNING.
THEY'RE INSIDE, MY KING.
I WAS WRONG ABOUT THEM.
TRISTAN HAS PLACED HIS SWORD BETWEEN THEM. NO TRUE KNIGHT WOULD CROSS OVER HIS SWORD. THAT WOULD BREAK HIS KNIGHTLY OATH.
MY KING. WHY ARE YOU HERE?
I DID NOT TRUST YOU. I WAS WRONG.
WILL YOU COME BACK AND BE MY KNIGHT AGAIN?
NO, I CANNOT.
I HAVE NOT BETRAYED YOU, BUT I DO LOVE ISOLDE.
I UNDERSTAND. BUT YOU HAVE COMMITTED NO SIN.
STILL, I WILL LEAVE. IT WILL STOP PEOPLE FROM ALWAYS QUESTIONING ISOLDE'S HONOR.
I ASK OF YOU ONLY ONE THING-
-TO HAVE ISOLDE'S RING TO REMEMBER HER BY.
YES, OF COURSE.

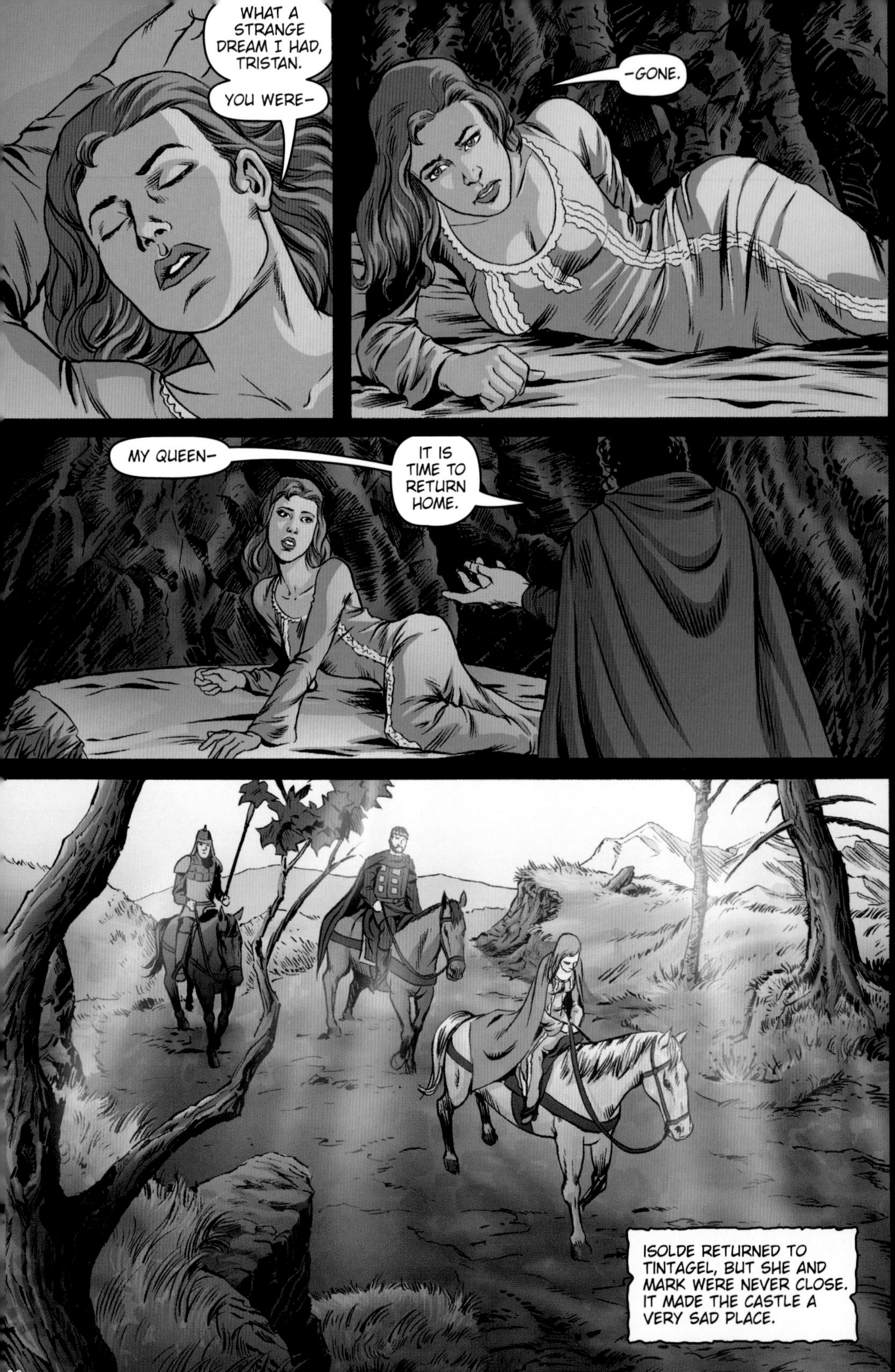
WHAT A STRANGE DREAM I HAD, TRISTAN.
YOU WERE-
-GONE.
MY QUEEN-
IT IS TIME TO RETURN HOME.
ISOLDE RETURNED TO TINTAGEL, BUT SHE AND MARK WERE NEVER CLOSE. IT MADE THE CASTLE A VERY SAD PLACE.

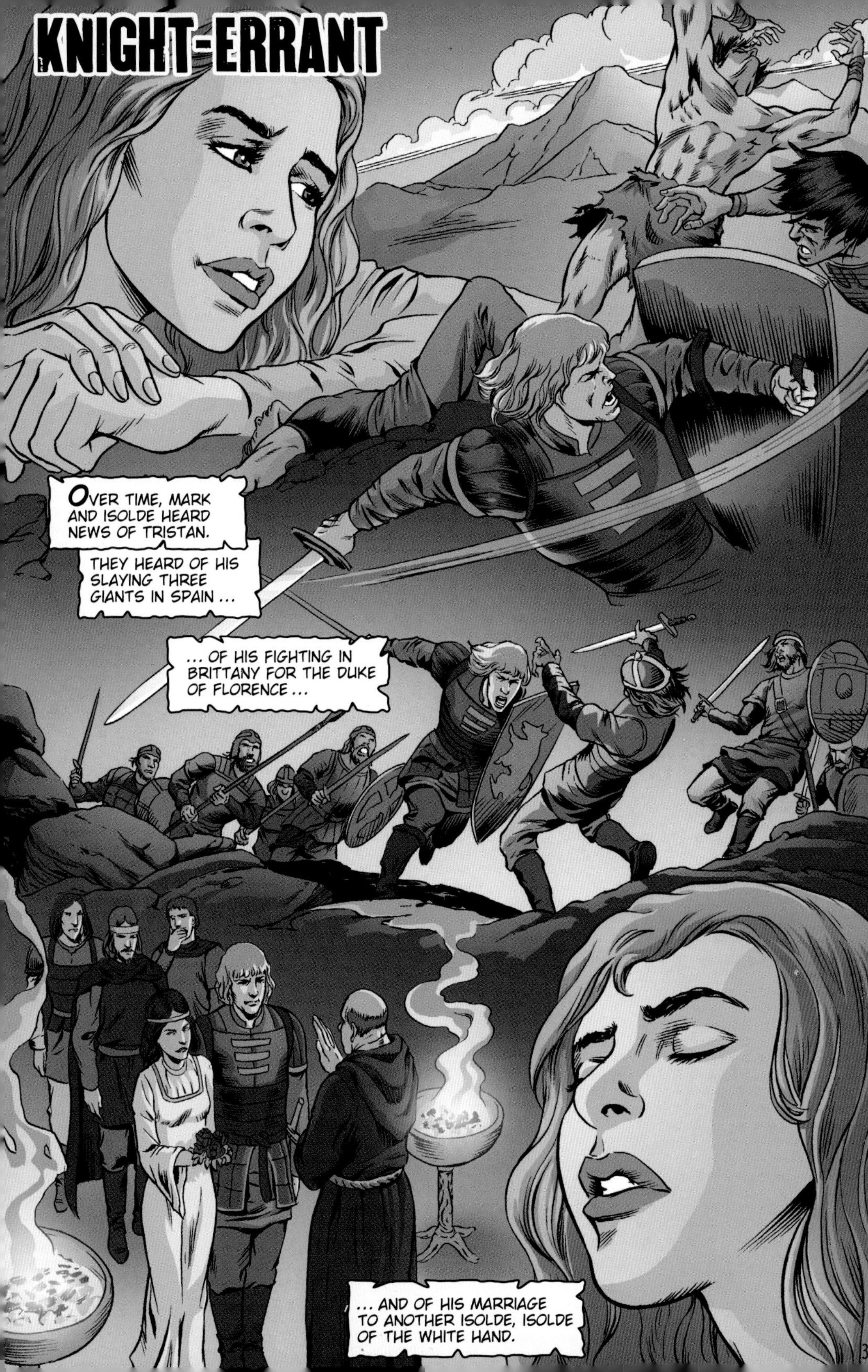
KNIGHT-ERRANT
OVER TIME, MARK AND ISOLDE HEARD NEWS OF TRISTAN.
THEY HEARD OF HIS SLAYING THREE GIANTS IN SPAIN ...
... OF HIS FIGHTING IN BRITTANY FOR THE DUKE OF FLORENCE ...
... AND OF HIS MARRIAGE TO ANOTHER ISOLDE, ISOLDE OF THE WHITE HAND.

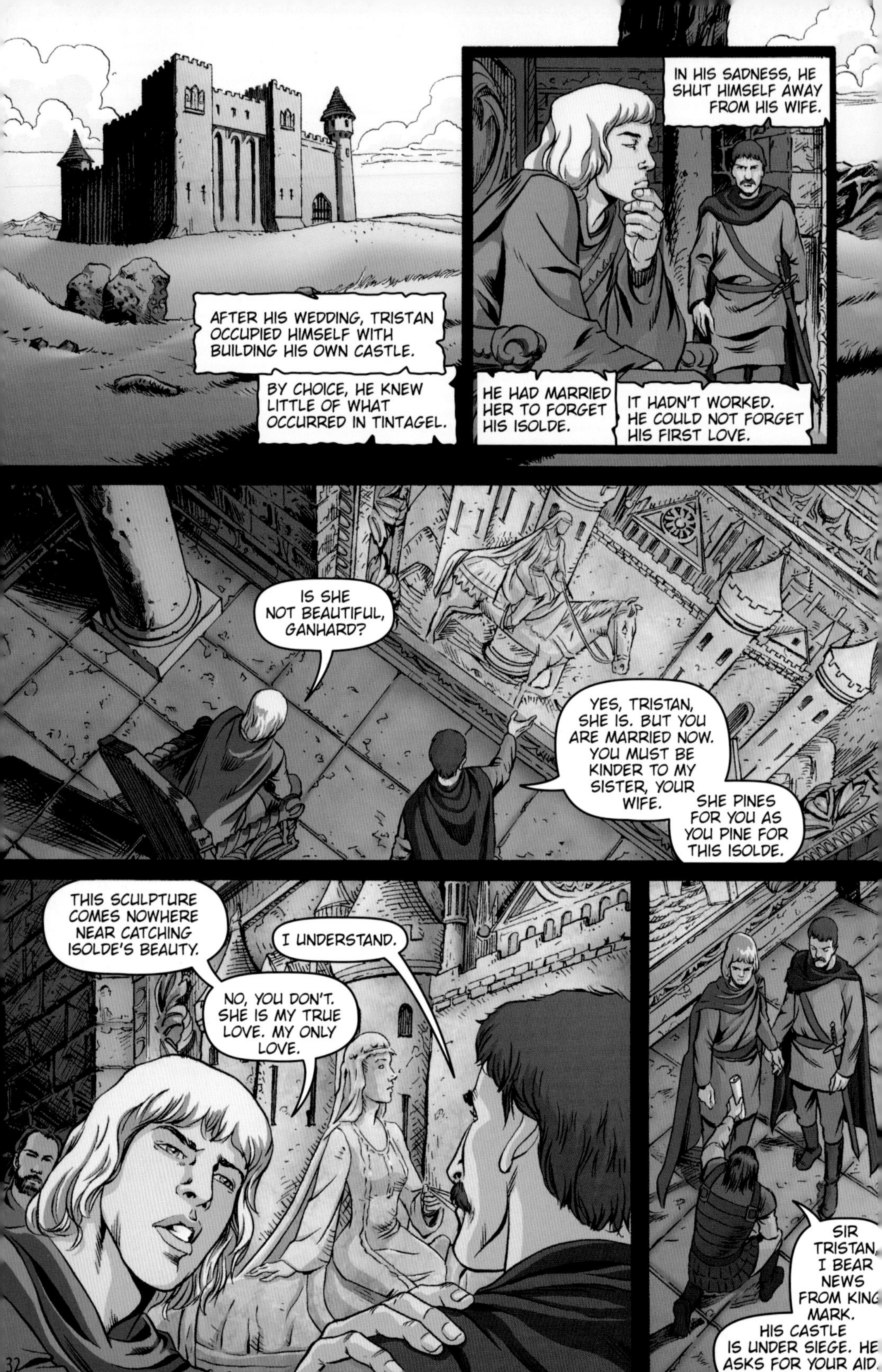
AFTER HIS WEDDING, TRISTAN OCCUPIED HIMSELF WITH BUILDING HIS OWN CASTLE.
BY CHOICE, HE KNEW LITTLE OF WHAT OCCURRED IN TINTAGEL.
IN HIS SADNESS, HE SHUT HIMSELF AWAY FROM HIS WIFE.
HE HAD MARRIED HER TO FORGET HIS ISOLDE.
IT HADN'T WORKED. HE COULD NOT FORGET HIS FIRST LOVE.
IS SHE NOT BEAUTIFUL, GANHARD?
YES, TRISTAN, SHE IS. BUT YOU ARE MARRIED NOW. YOU MUST BE KINDER TO MY SISTER, YOUR WIFE.
SHE PINES FOR YOU AS YOU PINE FOR THIS ISOLDE.
THIS SCULPTURE COMES NOWHERE NEAR CATCHING ISOLDE'S BEAUTY.
I UNDERSTAND.
NO, YOU DON'T. SHE IS MY TRUE LOVE. MY ONLY LOVE.
SIR TRISTAN, I BEAR NEWS FROM KING MARK. HIS CASTLE IS UNDER SIEGE. HE ASKS FOR YOUR AID.

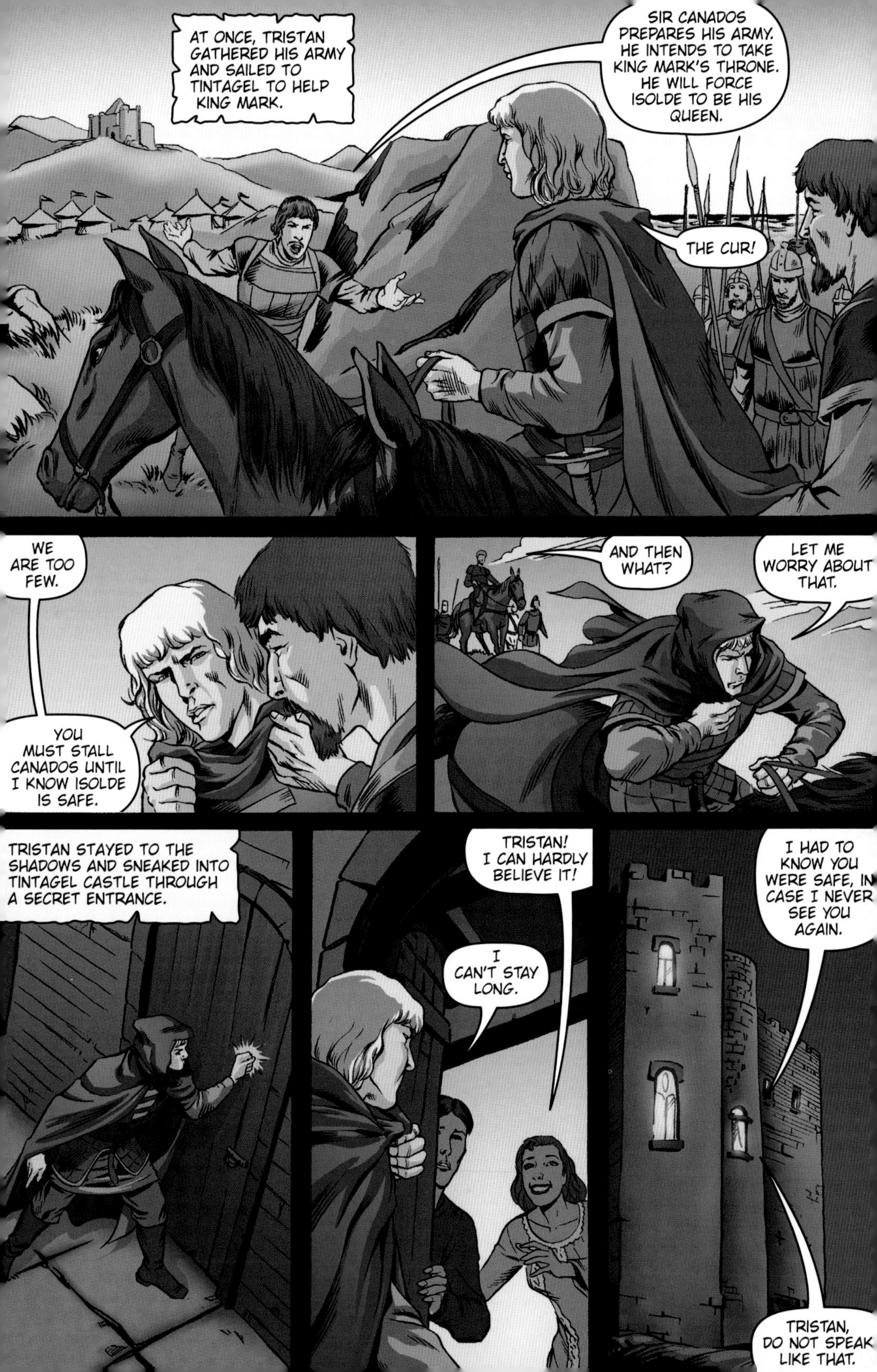
AT ONCE, TRISTAN GATHERED HIS ARMY AND SAILED TO TINTAGEL TO HELP KING MARK.
SIR CANADOS PREPARES HIS ARMY. HE INTENDS TO TAKE KING MARK'S THRONE. HE WILL FORCE ISOLDE TO BE HIS QUEEN.
THE CUR!
WE ARE TOO FEW.
YOU MUST STALL CANADOS UNTIL I KNOW ISOLDE IS SAFE.
AND THEN WHAT?
LET ME WORRY ABOUT THAT.
TRISTAN STAYED TO THE SHADOWS AND SNEAKED INTO TINTAGEL CASTLE THROUGH A SECRET ENTRANCE.
TRISTAN! I CAN HARDLY BELIEVE IT!
I CAN'T STAY LONG.
I HAD TO KNOW YOU WERE SAFE, IN CASE I NEVER SEE YOU AGAIN.
TRISTAN, DO NOT SPEAK LIKE THAT.

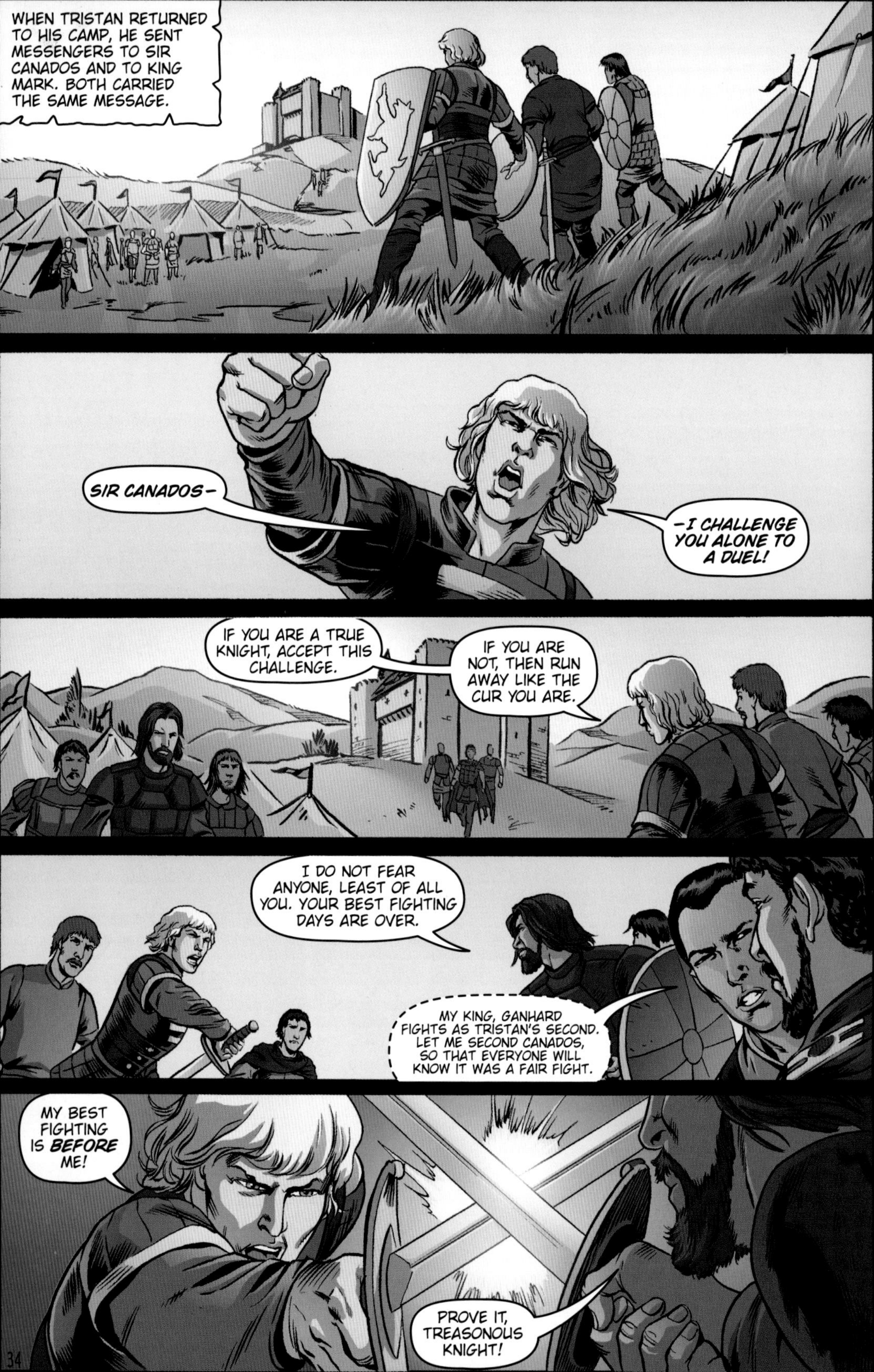
WHEN TRISTAN RETURNED TO HIS CAMP, HE SENT MESSENGERS TO SIR CANADOS AND TO KING MARK. BOTH CARRIED THE SAME MESSAGE.
SIR CANADOS–
–I CHALLENGE YOU ALONE TO A DUEL!
IF YOU ARE A TRUE KNIGHT, ACCEPT THIS CHALLENGE.
IF YOU ARE NOT, THEN RUN AWAY LIKE THE CUR YOU ARE.
I DO NOT FEAR ANYONE, LEAST OF ALL YOU. YOUR BEST FIGHTING DAYS ARE OVER.
MY KING, GANHARD FIGHTS AS TRISTAN'S SECOND. LET ME SECOND CANADOS, SO THAT EVERYONE WILL KNOW IT WAS A FAIR FIGHT.
MY BEST FIGHTING IS *BEFORE* ME!
PROVE IT, TREASONOUS KNIGHT!

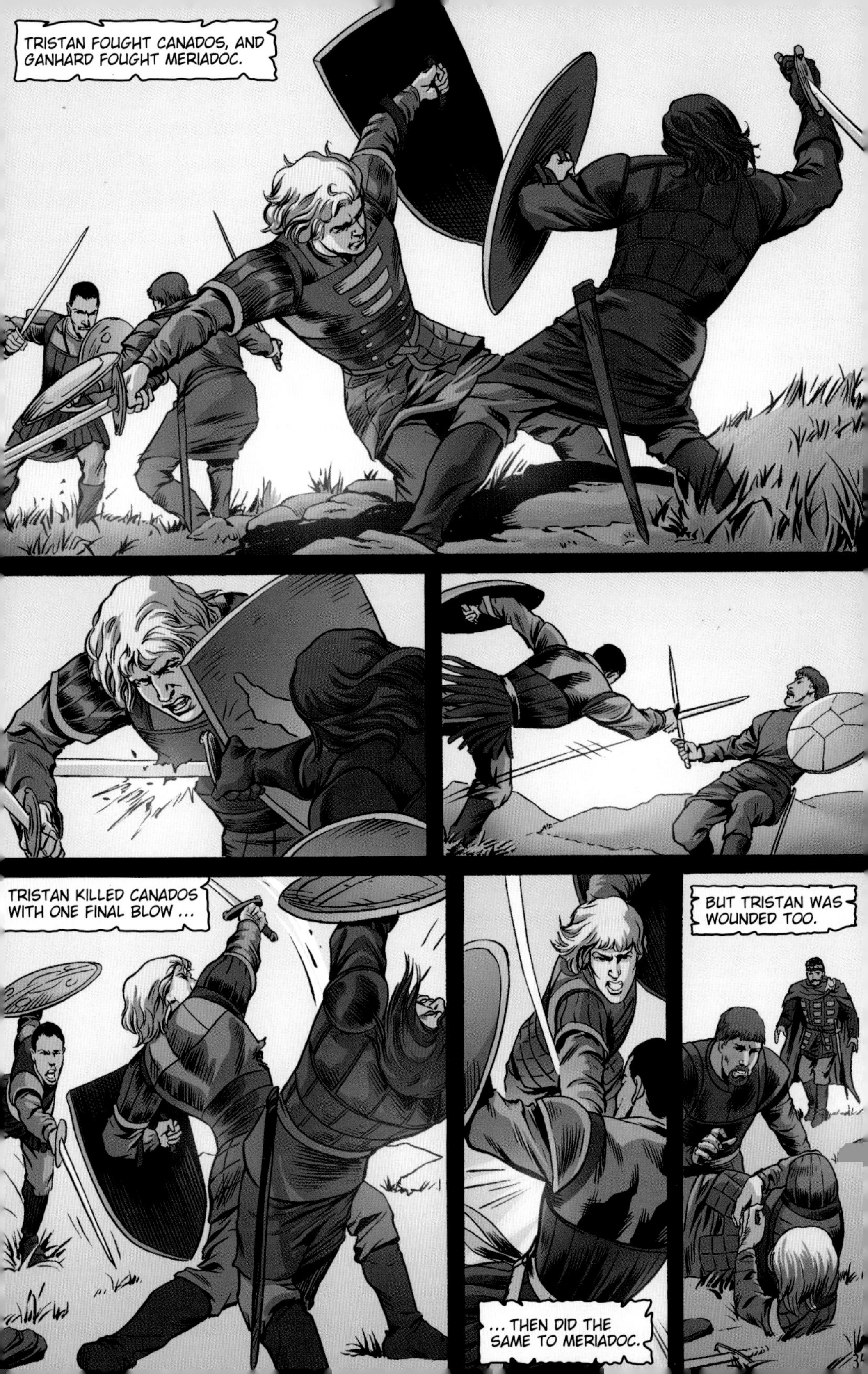
TRISTAN FOUGHT CANADOS, AND GANHARD FOUGHT MERIADOC.
TRISTAN KILLED CANADOS WITH ONE FINAL BLOW ...
... THEN DID THE SAME TO MERIADOC.
BUT TRISTAN WAS WOUNDED TOO.

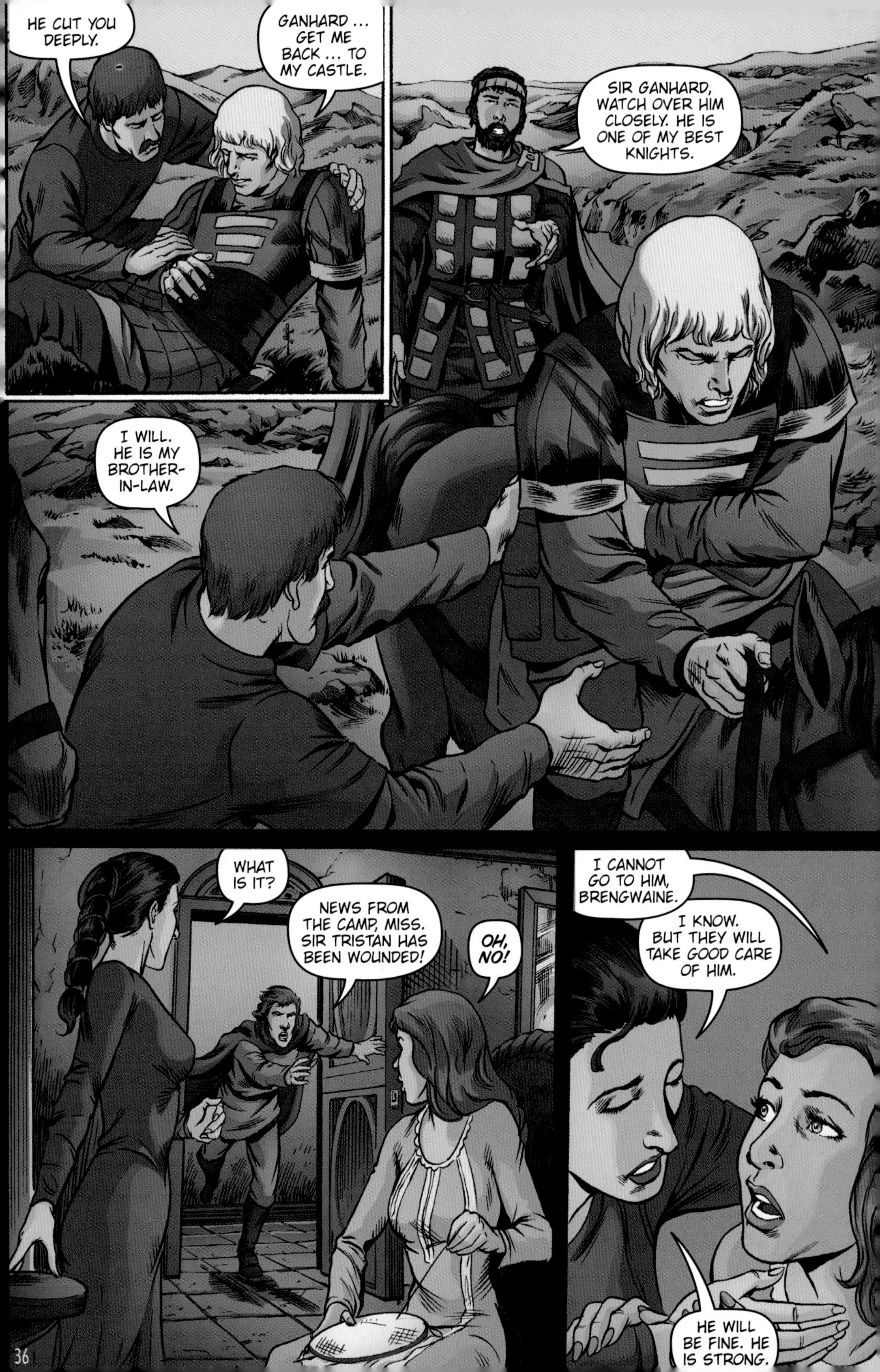
HE CUT YOU DEEPLY.
GANHARD ... GET ME BACK ... TO MY CASTLE.
SIR GANHARD, WATCH OVER HIM CLOSELY. HE IS ONE OF MY BEST KNIGHTS.
I WILL. HE IS MY BROTHER-IN-LAW.
WHAT IS IT?
NEWS FROM THE CAMP, MISS. SIR TRISTAN HAS BEEN WOUNDED!
OH, NO!
I CANNOT GO TO HIM, BRENGWAINE.
I KNOW. BUT THEY WILL TAKE GOOD CARE OF HIM.
HE WILL BE FINE. HE IS STRONG.

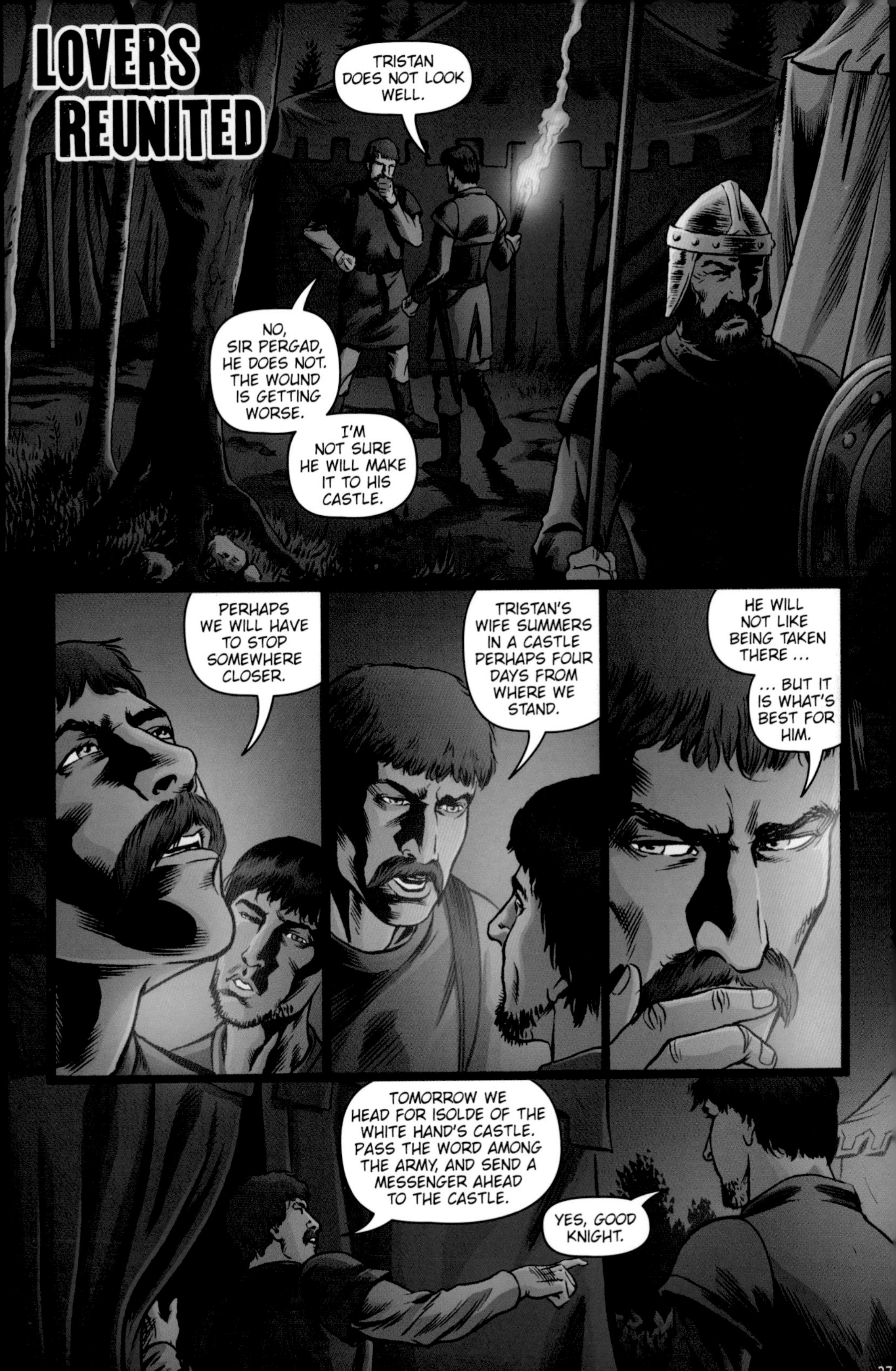
LOVERS REUNITED
TRISTAN DOES NOT LOOK WELL.
NO, SIR PERGAD, HE DOES NOT. THE WOUND IS GETTING WORSE.
I'M NOT SURE HE WILL MAKE IT TO HIS CASTLE.
PERHAPS WE WILL HAVE TO STOP SOMEWHERE CLOSER.
TRISTAN'S WIFE SUMMERS IN A CASTLE PERHAPS FOUR DAYS FROM WHERE WE STAND.
HE WILL NOT LIKE BEING TAKEN THERE ...
... BUT IT IS WHAT'S BEST FOR HIM.
TOMORROW WE HEAD FOR ISOLDE OF THE WHITE HAND'S CASTLE. PASS THE WORD AMONG THE ARMY, AND SEND A MESSENGER AHEAD TO THE CASTLE.
YES, GOOD KNIGHT.

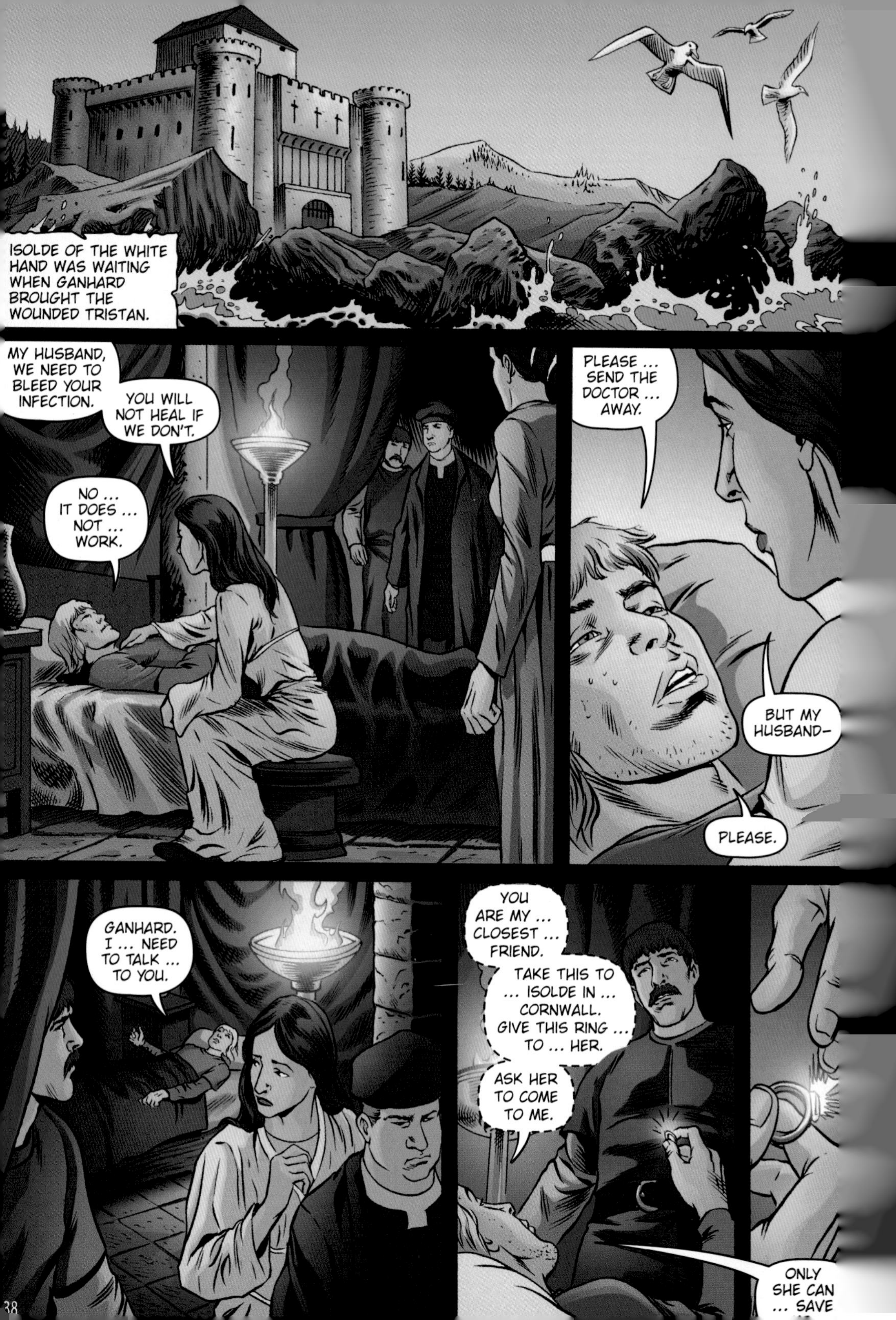
ISOLDE OF THE WHITE HAND WAS WAITING WHEN GANHARD BROUGHT THE WOUNDED TRISTAN.
MY HUSBAND, WE NEED TO BLEED YOUR INFECTION.
YOU WILL NOT HEAL IF WE DON'T.
NO ... IT DOES ... NOT ... WORK.
PLEASE ... SEND THE DOCTOR ... AWAY.
BUT MY HUSBAND-
PLEASE.
GANHARD. I ... NEED TO TALK ... TO YOU.
YOU ARE MY ... CLOSEST ... FRIEND.
TAKE THIS TO ... ISOLDE IN ... CORNWALL. GIVE THIS RING ... TO ... HER.
ASK HER TO COME TO ME.
ONLY SHE CAN ... SAVE

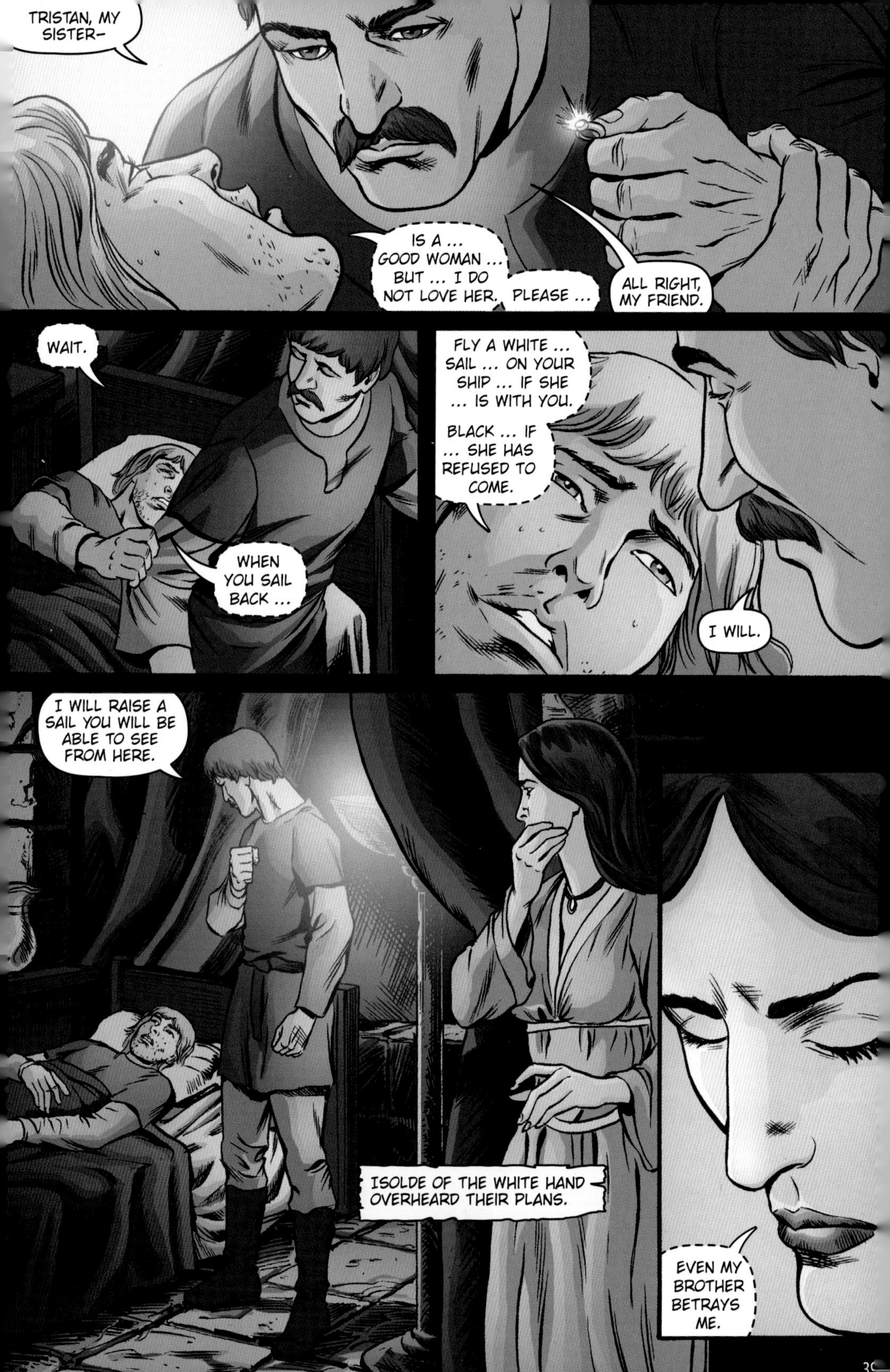
TRISTAN, MY SISTER-
IS A ... GOOD WOMAN ... BUT ... I DO NOT LOVE HER.
PLEASE ...
ALL RIGHT, MY FRIEND.
WAIT.
WHEN YOU SAIL BACK ...
FLY A WHITE ... SAIL ... ON YOUR SHIP ... IF SHE ... IS WITH YOU.
BLACK ... IF ... SHE HAS REFUSED TO COME.
I WILL.
I WILL RAISE A SAIL YOU WILL BE ABLE TO SEE FROM HERE.
ISOLDE OF THE WHITE HAND OVERHEARD THEIR PLANS.
EVEN MY BROTHER BETRAYS ME.

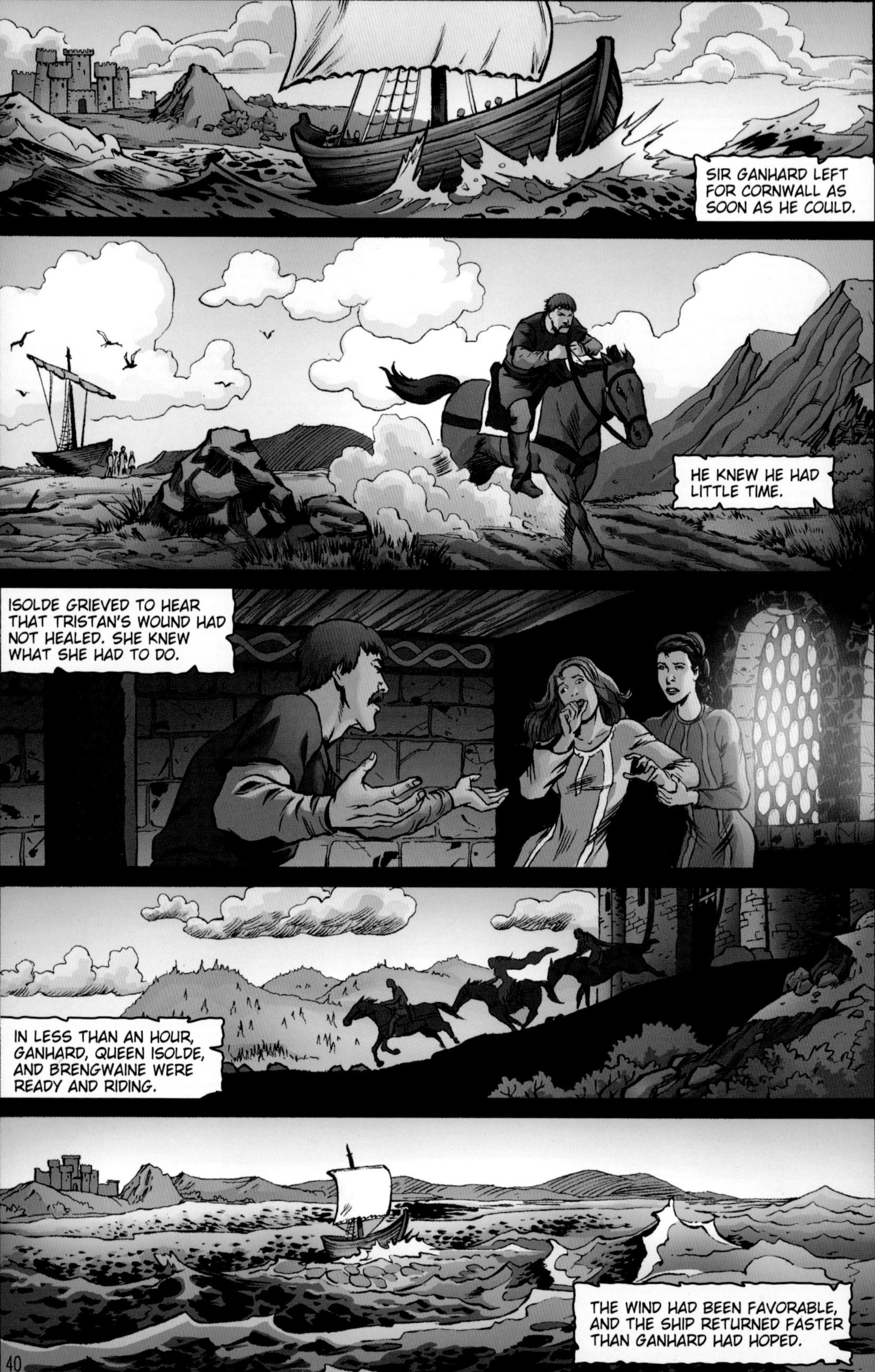

SIR GANHARD LEFT FOR CORNWALL AS SOON AS HE COULD.
HE KNEW HE HAD LITTLE TIME.
ISOLDE GRIEVED TO HEAR THAT TRISTAN'S WOUND HAD NOT HEALED. SHE KNEW WHAT SHE HAD TO DO.
IN LESS THAN AN HOUR, GANHARD, QUEEN ISOLDE, AND BRENGWAINE WERE READY AND RIDING.
THE WIND HAD BEEN FAVORABLE, AND THE SHIP RETURNED FASTER THAN GANHARD HAD HOPED.

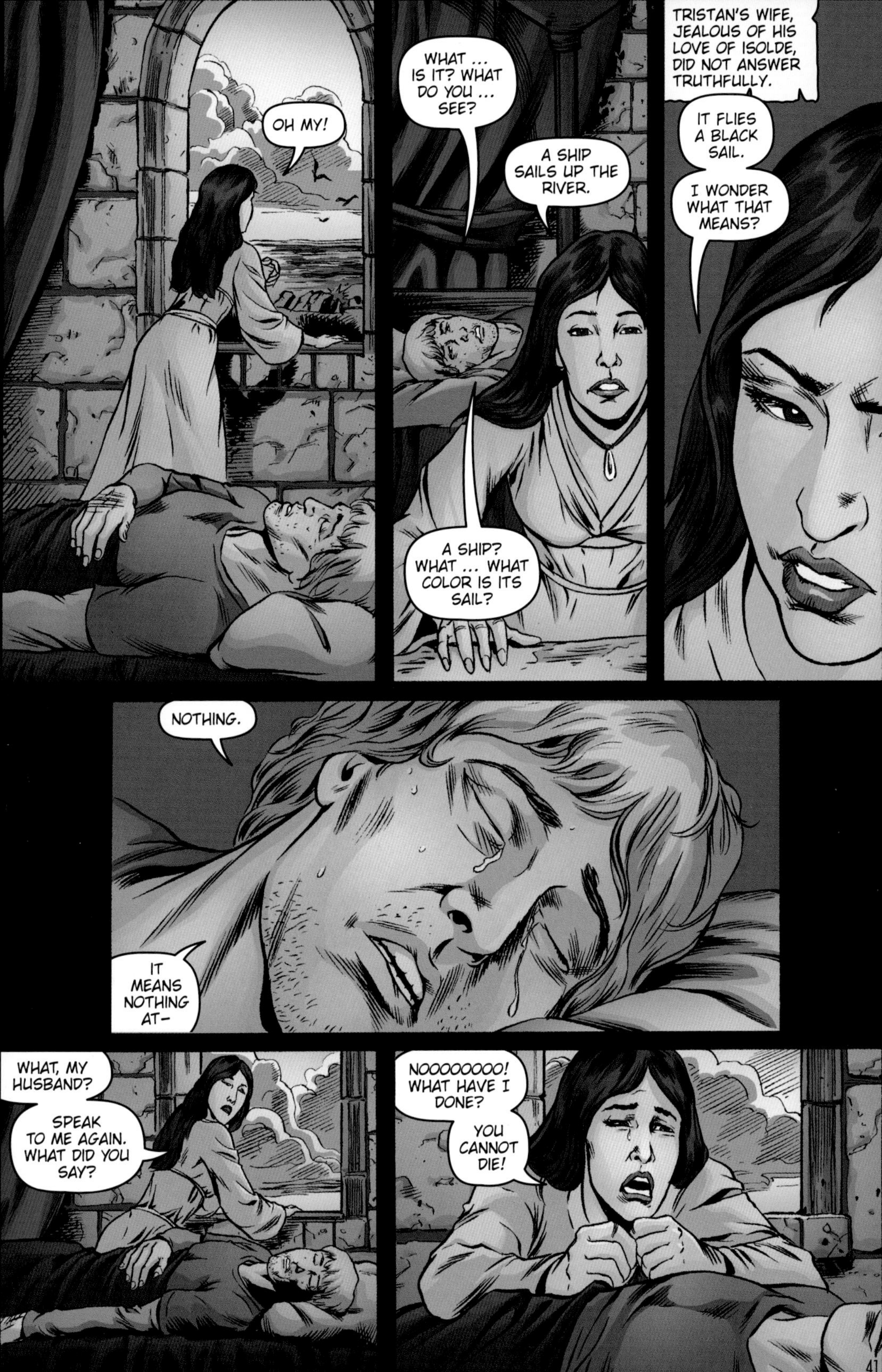
OH MY!
WHAT ... IS IT? WHAT DO YOU ... SEE?
A SHIP SAILS UP THE RIVER.
A SHIP? WHAT ... WHAT COLOR IS ITS SAIL?
TRISTAN'S WIFE, JEALOUS OF HIS LOVE OF ISOLDE, DID NOT ANSWER TRUTHFULLY.
IT FLIES A BLACK SAIL.
I WONDER WHAT THAT MEANS?
NOTHING.
IT MEANS NOTHING AT-
WHAT, MY HUSBAND?
SPEAK TO ME AGAIN. WHAT DID YOU SAY?
NOOOOOOOO! WHAT HAVE I DONE?
YOU CANNOT DIE!

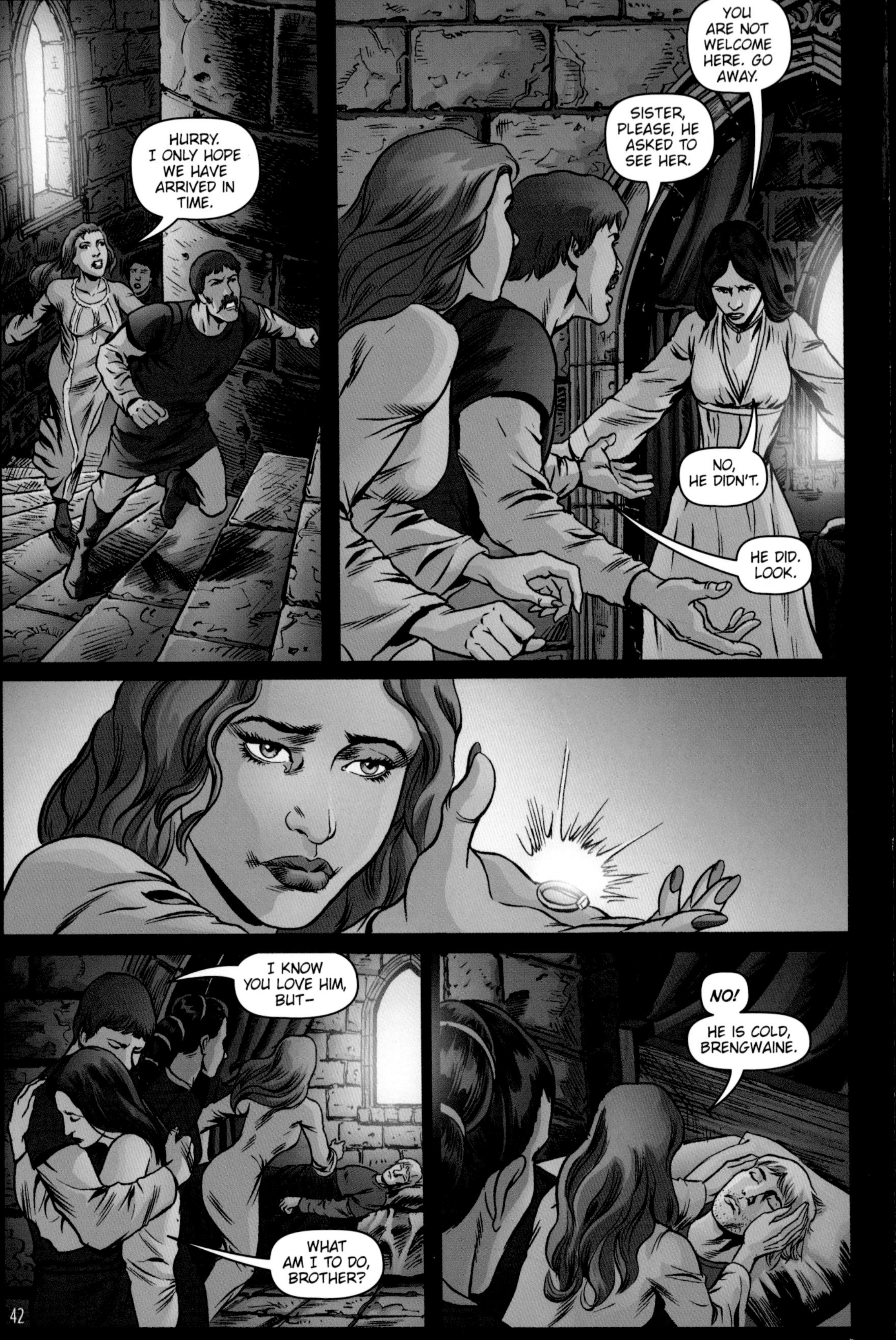
HURRY. I ONLY HOPE WE HAVE ARRIVED IN TIME.
YOU ARE NOT WELCOME HERE. GO AWAY.
SISTER, PLEASE, HE ASKED TO SEE HER.
NO, HE DIDN'T.
HE DID. LOOK.
I KNOW YOU LOVE HIM, BUT-
WHAT AM I TO DO, BROTHER?
NO!
HE IS COLD, BRENGWAINE.

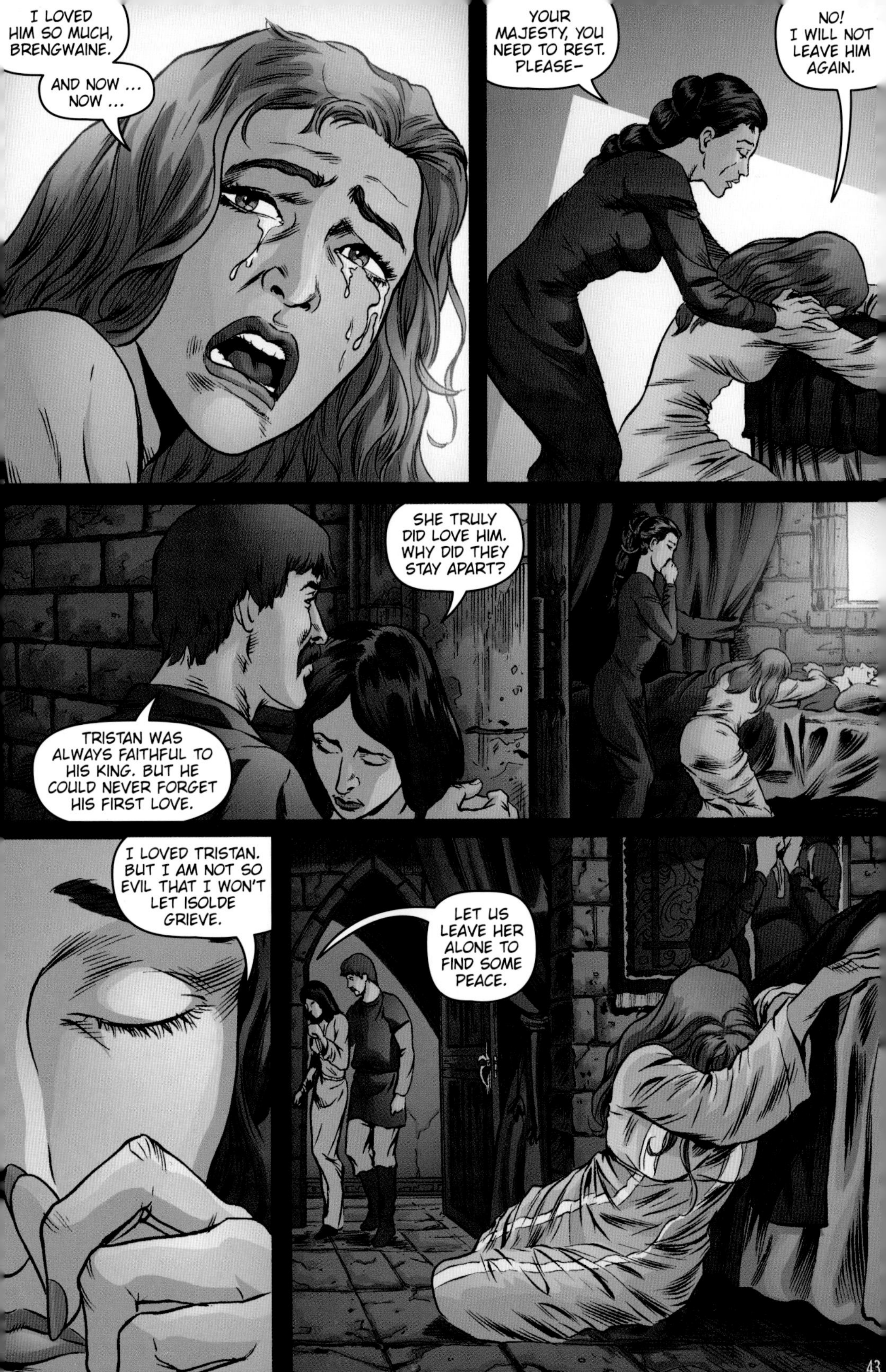
I LOVED HIM SO MUCH, BRENGWAINE.
AND NOW ... NOW ...
YOUR MAJESTY, YOU NEED TO REST. PLEASE-
NO! I WILL NOT LEAVE HIM AGAIN.
SHE TRULY DID LOVE HIM. WHY DID THEY STAY APART?
TRISTAN WAS ALWAYS FAITHFUL TO HIS KING. BUT HE COULD NEVER FORGET HIS FIRST LOVE.
I LOVED TRISTAN. BUT I AM NOT SO EVIL THAT I WON'T LET ISOLDE GRIEVE.
LET US LEAVE HER ALONE TO FIND SOME PEACE.

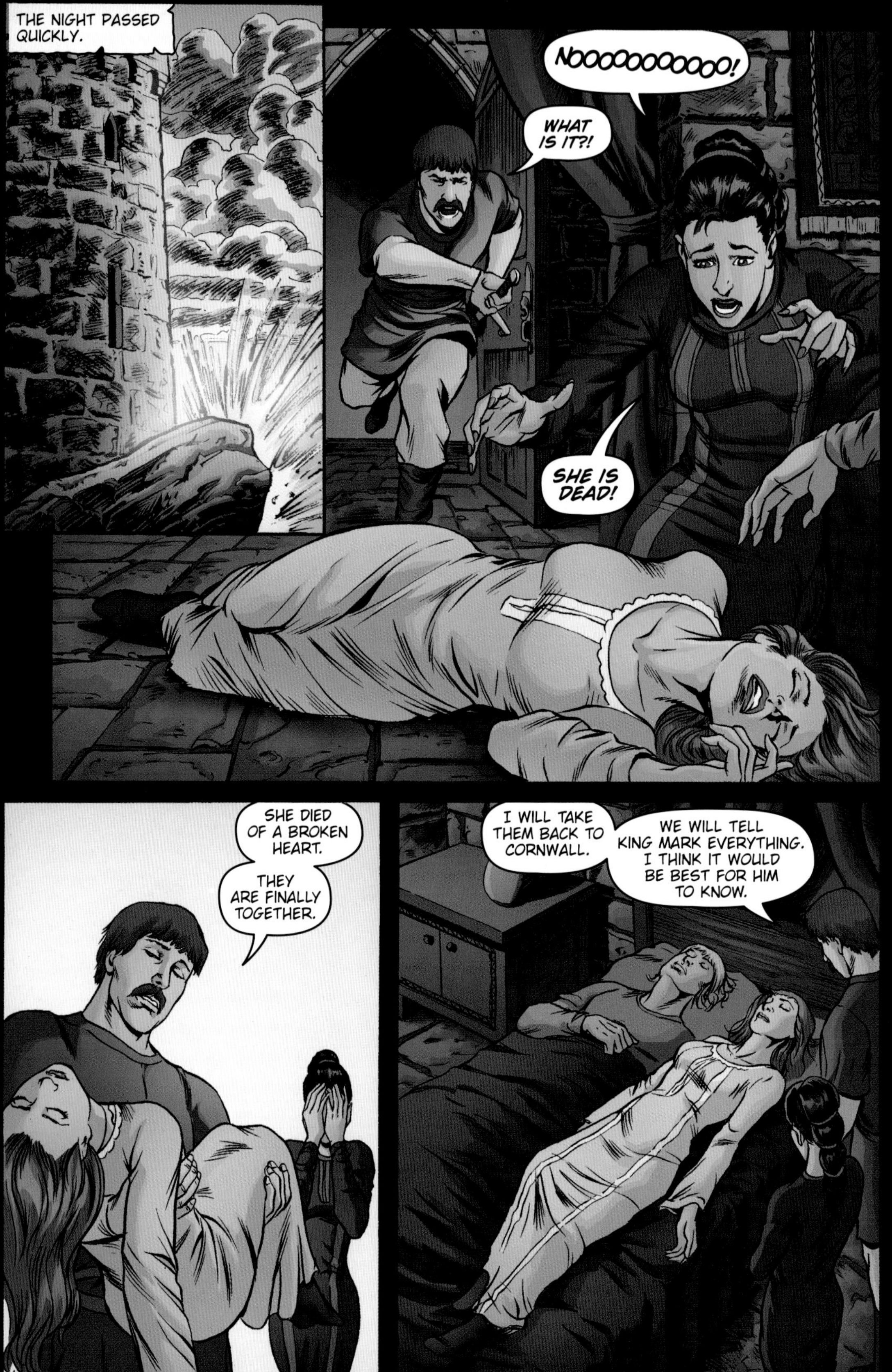
THE NIGHT PASSED QUICKLY.
NOOOOOOOOOOO!
WHAT IS IT?!
SHE IS DEAD!
SHE DIED OF A BROKEN HEART.
THEY ARE FINALLY TOGETHER.
I WILL TAKE THEM BACK TO CORNWALL.
WE WILL TELL KING MARK EVERYTHING. I THINK IT WOULD BE BEST FOR HIM TO KNOW.
44

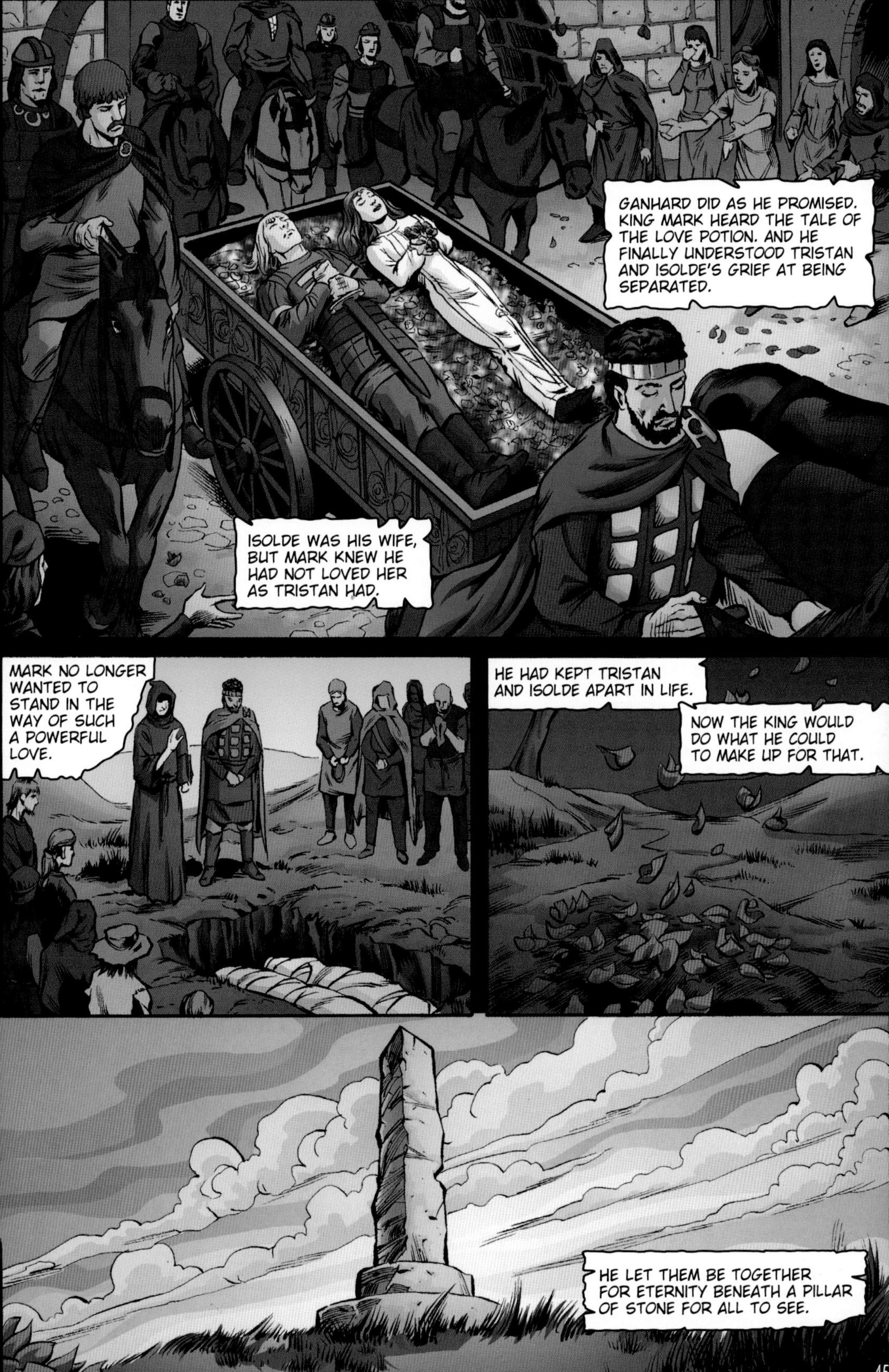
GANHARD DID AS HE PROMISED. KING MARK HEARD THE TALE OF THE LOVE POTION. AND HE FINALLY UNDERSTOOD TRISTAN AND ISOLDE'S GRIEF AT BEING SEPARATED.
ISOLDE WAS HIS WIFE, BUT MARK KNEW HE HAD NOT LOVED HER AS TRISTAN HAD.
MARK NO LONGER WANTED TO STAND IN THE WAY OF SUCH A POWERFUL LOVE.
HE HAD KEPT TRISTAN AND ISOLDE APART IN LIFE.
NOW THE KING WOULD DO WHAT HE COULD TO MAKE UP FOR THAT.
HE LET THEM BE TOGETHER FOR ETERNITY BENEATH A PILLAR OF STONE FOR ALL TO SEE.

GLOSSARY AND PRONUNCIATION GUIDE

ANGUIN (AN-gwin): an Irish king and Isolde's father

BRENGWAINE (BREN-gwayn): Isolde's lady-in-waiting

CORNWALL: a county on the southwestern tip of England. Until the early Middle Ages, Cornwall was ruled by chieftains and minor kings.

COURT: the place from which a sovereign (such as a king) rules. The term also refers to the family, advisers, and friends of the king who attend him at court.

ERRANT: wandering or traveling. A knight-errant was a knight who traveled from place to place looking for adventures or offering his services as a soldier.

ISEULT (ih-ZOOLT): an Irish queen and the mother of Isolde

ISOLDE (ih-ZOHL-duh): an Irish princess and the wife of King Mark of Cornwall

KNIGHT: a mounted soldier sworn to loyally serve a lord or ruler. In the Middle Ages, when a man became a knight, he swore an oath. He promised to obey religious law, defend the weak, honor women, serve his king, and protect his country.

LADY-IN-WAITING: a woman who serves a queen or a princess

LORD: a ruler or landowner with authority over a group of people

MERIADOC (MEHR-ee-ah-dahk): a knight in King Mark's court

PEASANT: a person of low birth

SECOND: a person who assists another during a duel or a fight

SIEGE (seej): a military attack on a castle or fort, to force the occupants to surrender

STEWARD: a servant in a castle or a large house. Stewards usually had a high rank among the servants.

TINTAGEL (tin-TAH-jel): King Mark's castle. Tintagel is a real castle on the north coast of Cornwall, England. It has been linked to Arthurian legend since the twelfth century A.D.

TREASON: the crime of betraying a sovereign (such as a king), which is seen as endangering the order and the safety of the kingdom

TRISTAN (TRIS-tuhn): a knight and the nephew of King Mark

WINE SACK: a pouch, often made of animal skin, with a top that closed, made for carrying wine

FURTHER READING AND WEBSITES

Crosley-Holland, Kevin. *The World of King Arthur and His Court: People, Places, Legend and Lore.* New York: Dutton Books, 2004. An illustrated guide providing information on key characters, daily life in a castle, knighthood, and other aspects of Arthurian legend.

King Arthur
http://tlc.discovery.com/convergence/arthur/arthur.html
The Learning Channel's website features a gallery of Arthurian images, an interactive section on the legend of Arthur, and a timeline of Britain in the Dark Ages.

King Arthur and the Knights of the Round Table
http://www.kingarthursknights.com
This website provides articles on the historical and legendary Arthur, a map and information on Arthurian sites, artwork, and the stories of the knights and other characters of the famous legend.

CREATING *TRISTAN & ISOLDE*

In creating this story, author Jeff Limke used Thomas Malory's *Le Morte d'Arthur* and *Popular Romances of the Middle Ages* by George Cox and Eustace Jones. Artist Ron Randall used many historical and traditional sources to shape the story's visual details. Consultant Theresa Krier used her knowledge of Arthurian lore and medieval culture to ensure accuracy.

original pencil sketch from page 31

INDEX

Anguin (Isolde's father), 10; sends Isolde to Cornwall to marry Mark, 11

Brengwaine: mixes up wine and love potion, 13

Canados, 33; fights Tristan, 34-35
Cornwall, 6, 10, 11, 12, 15, 25, 38, 44

Ganhard, 32, 33; brings Isolde to Tristan, 39-40; as Tristan's second, 34-36, 37

Ireland, 6, 7-12, 13
Iseult (Isolde's mother): curing powers of, 9, 10; gives Brengwaine love potion, 12
Isolde: death of, 44; falls in love with Tristan, 14; finds wounded Tristan on road, 9-10; marries Mark, 15
Isolde of the White Hand, 32, 37, 38; lies about ship's sails, 41; marries Tristan, 31

knightly oath, 29

Llud, 6, 16, 20, 22, 28

Mark: adoption of Tristan, 6; banishes Tristan, 18; forgives Tristan and Isolde, 26, 29, 45; marries Isolde, 15; sentences Isolde to death, 24
Meriadoc, 16; accuses Isolde of affair with Tristan, 18-19; sets traps for Tristan, 21, 22
Moraunt, 7, 11

steward: claims he killed dragon, 8-9; lies to King Anguin, 12

Tintagel Castle, 6, 15, 31, 32; under siege by Canados, 33
Tristan: death of, 41; falls in love with Isolde, 14; marries Isolde of the White Hand, 32; poisoned by Moraunt, 6-7; rescues Isolde from execution, 24-25; slays Irish dragon, 7-8; wounded by Canados, 35-36

ABOUT THE AUTHOR AND THE ARTIST

JEFF LIMKE was raised in North Dakota, where he first read, listened to, and marveled at Arthurian tales of knights and their adventures. Limke later taught these stories for many years and has written several adaptations of them. His Graphic Myths and Legends work includes *King Arthur: Excalibur Unsheathed*, *Isis & Osiris: To the Ends of the Earth*, *Thor & Loki: In the Land of Giants*, *Jason: Quest for the Golden Fleece*, *Theseus: Battling the Minotaur*, and *Arthur & Lancelot: The Fight for Camelot*. Other stories have been published by Caliber Comics, Arrow Comics, and Kenzer and Company.

RON RANDALL has drawn comics for every major comic book publisher in the United States, including Marvel, DC, Image, and Dark Horse. His Graphic Myths and Legends work includes *Thor & Loki: In the Land of Giants*, *Amaterasu: Return of the Sun*, *Beowulf: Monster Slayer*, and *Guan Yu: Blood Brothers to the End*. He has also worked on superhero comics such as Justice League and Spiderman; science fiction titles such as *Star Wars* and *Star Trek*; fantasy adventure titles such as *DragonLance* and *Warlord*; suspense and horror titles including *SwampThing*, *Predator*, and *Venom*; and his own creation, *Trekker*.